The Word Finder

The Word Finder

Albert and Joan Rowe

BASIL BLACKWELL

Books by Albert Rowe

Active Anthologies, Books 1-3
British Teaching and its Contribution to Secondary Education
Desk Book of Plain English
English for Living, Books 1 − 4
English Through Experience, Books 1 − 5 (with Peter Emmens)
Federico García Lorca: Lyrics and Shorter Poems (translation)
Federico García Lorca, the Man and his Poetry
Language Links
Language Skills
Let's Laugh: Topliner Book of Humour
People Like Us: Short Stories for Secondary Schools
Poems   Federico García Lorca (translation)
Pollen Girl: Rockets
Positive English, Books 1-4
St Ives Boy's Summer and Other Poems
The Education of the Average Child
The Harmonica and Recorder Teacher's Manual (with Gareth Walters)
The Quest of Julian Day (adapted)
The School as a Guidance Community
Twenty Poems of Love and a Song of Desperation by Pablo Neruda
  (translation)

© Albert Rowe 1983

First published 1983

Published by
Basil Blackwell Publisher
108 Cowley Rd
Oxford OX4 1JF

British Library Cataloguing in Publication Data

Rowe, Albert
  The Word Finder
  1. English language
  Juvenile literature
  I. Title   II. Rowe, Joan
  423'.1   PE1591

ISBN 0 631 13201 5 hardback   ISBN 0 631 91950 3 paperback

Typesetting in 10/11 Paladium by Getset (BTS) Ltd, Eynsham, Oxford
Printed in Great Britain

To the Student

This book has been written to help you to choose the word that expresses your meaning exactly rather than write the first word that comes into your head.

It consists of 804 numbered headwords printed in **bold** type, and more than 7,000 related words. The headwords are among the commonest words we use when we write. Below each are a number of related words from which we can choose the word we wish to use if we do not wish to use the headword itself.

The words below each headword are as follows:

1 Synonyms. These are not defined because they mean the same, or nearly the same, as the headword itself.

2 Alternatives. These are in italics. They are closely related to the headword. The meaning of each is carefully defined to help you to make up your mind which you would like to use.

3 Extensions. These are also in italics and widen your choice still further. Most you will know, but some you will need to look up in your dictionary.

The Index lists all the words in their alphabetical order. Use it to look up the word you are thinking of using, then study the headword section in which it appears to choose the word that will best express your meaning.

1 **abandon** v.

desert leave

discard put aside as unwanted
get rid of throw away
jettison throw goods overboard to
  lighten a ship in distress
leave go away from
relinquish give up, usually to give up
  possession

forsake *surrender*

2 **ability** n.

capability capacity

aptitude natural ability, especially in
  learning
cleverness quickness in learning, or
  skill in using hands or body
gift special aptitude
potential possibility for developing
  or being developed
power vigour, energy, strength
talent special or very great ability

endowment *ingenuity* *mastery*

3 **abolish** v.

annul cancel; declare invalid
nullify cause or declare to have no
  effect
repeal cancel, especially in law
retract take back a statement or offer
  made
revoke withdraw or cancel a decree
  or licence
supersede replace, especially as an
  improvement on

eradicate

4 **about** prep.

concerning regarding respecting

dealing with

5 **about to** prep.

prepared to *ready to* *soon to*

6 **about** adv. and prep.

approximately more or less roughly

approaching *close to*

7 **above** adv.

at the top *high up* *on high*
overhead

8 **absolutely** adv.

certainly completely fully totally
unconditionally utterly wholly

9 **abuse** v. (i)

misapply misuse

exploit use a person unfairly for one's
  own profit
impose on take unfair advantage of

take advantage of

10 **abuse** v. (ii)

rail against complain or protest
  about; reproach strongly
revile criticize angrily in abusive
  language

11 **accept** v.

get come into possession of
receive take in something sent or
  given
take get possession of

abide by *agree to* *assent to*
comply with *take on*

12 **acceptable** adj.

commendable worthy of praise
proper suitable, correct
respectable having character and
  standards suited to society
worthy deserving respect or support

adequate all right fitting

13 **accident** n.

misadventure mischance misfortune

disaster sudden or great misfortune

calamity catastrophe

14 **accidental** adj.

unintentional unplanned unpremeditated

chance unplanned; happening by
  luck or fate
haphazard happening in a disorderly
  manner
unforeseen unexpected

15 **accuse** v.

charge

allege state or declare without proof
censure express strong disapproval
impute attribute wrongdoing to
  someone

16 **across** prep.

*confronting facing fronting
on the other side of opposite to
over*

17 **across** adv.

*astraddle astride crosswise
transversely*

18 **act** n.

action deed

conduct behaviour
performance notable action; carrying
  out

enterprise exploit

19 **act** v.

assume take on or undertake
behave bear oneself in an acceptable
  way
feign put on a false air
pretend give a deceiving appearance

fake sham

20 **addicted** adj.

dedicated to working hard for a
  special purpose
dependent on unable to do without
devoted to loving or loyal to a
  particular activity or person
hooked obsessed by, usually drugs

21 **admire** v.

look up to think highly of

esteem respect greatly
honour show or feel great respect
respect think highly of
revere feel awe for
venerate honour as hallowed or
  sacred

22 **adult** adj.

*full-grown fully developed
grown-up mature*

23 **advise** v.

counsel

enjoin order or command

guide   influence strongly
recommend   offer as the best course
suggest   propose for acceptance or
  rejection
urge   beg or persuade strongly

prescribe

24   **affair**   n.

*business   episode   happening   pro-
ceedings   transaction   undertaking*

25   **affect**   v. (i)

influence

change   cause to become different
impress upon   make the importance
  of something clear
modify   make partial changes in
play on   make use of a person's
  sympathy for one's own advantage
sway   have influence over

26   **affect**   v. (ii)

move   stir   touch

agitate   cause anxiety to
hurt   cause pain to a person's feelings
perturb   make anxious or uneasy
soften   make less able to resist
impress   make an impression on; have
  a favourable effect on

inflict

27   **afraid**   adj.

alarmed   fearful   frightened   scared

apprehensive   feeling anxious,
  especially about the future
cowardly   unable to face danger,
  pain, or hardship
jittery   feeling anxious before an event
nervous   easily agitated
panic-stricken   filled with uncontrollable fear

terrified   filled with very great fear
timid   easily alarmed; lacking courage

craven   timorous

28   **afterwards**   adv.

later   subsequently   then

29   **again**   adv.
another time

afresh   anew

30   **agile**   adj.
nimble   well-coordinated

spry   active and brisk
supple   bending easily

light-footed

31   **agree**   v. (i)
consent

accept   take willingly; take as true
admit   accept as true or based on
  truth
allow   agree that something is true or
  acceptable
approve   feel that something is good
  or suitable
grant   agree that something is true

concur   reconcile

32   **agree**   v. (ii)
correspond

be appropriate   be suitable or proper
fit   be right and proper; be well
  adapted
match   equal in ability, skill, or
  appearance
resemble   be like

suit   satisfy or please; be convenient
  for
tally   correspond; be similar

coincide   conform

33 **aim**   n.
goal   object   purpose

ambition   strong desire to achieve
  something
plan   considered arrangement for
  some future activity
resolution   something one intends to
  do; mental pledge

intention   endeavour

34 **alert**   adj.
wide-awake

attentive   taking careful notice;
  listening carefully
prepared   ready to do something
vigilant   continually watchful
watchful   careful to notice things

heedful   prudent

35 **alive**   adj.
active   energetic

bustling   full of noisy activity
dynamic   full of power and activity
spirited   displaying vigour
sprightly   gay and full of energy
vital   full of life and force

36 **all**   adj.
complete   entire   total

37 **allow**   v.
let   permit   give permission

approve of   agree officially to
authorize   give power to or
  permission for

grant   permit what is requested
put up with   suffer without
  complaining
tolerate   permit without protest or
  interference

38 **almost**   adv.
nearly

*all but   close to   just about
not quite   virtually   wellnigh*

39 **also**   adv. & conj.
as well

*additionally   in addition
including   plus   too*

40 **although**   conj.
*even if   even though   granting that
in spite of the fact that   though*

41 **altogether**   adv.
*completely   entirely   totally
wholly*

42 **always**   adv.
*at all times   constantly   endlessly
eternally   everlastingly   evermore
every time   for ever
on every occasion   perpetually
unceasingly   without end*

43 **among**   prep.
*amid   amongst   in the middle of
in the thick of   surrounded by*

44 **amount**   n.
sum   total

aggregate   a mass or total made up of
  small parts

lot   a great quantity
number   a symbol or word indicating
  how many
quantity   an amount or number

45   **angle**   n.

*approach   attitude   point of view
standpoint*

46   **angry**   adj.

irate

annoyed   slightly angry
enraged   very angry
frantic   wildly agitated by anxiety
frenzied   state of wild, uncontrolled
  feeling
infuriated   intensely angry
irritable   tending to get angry over
  small things
raging   violently angry
ranting   talking in a loud, excited, or
  hostile way
raving   talking in a nonsensical or
  mad way

*cross   incensed   indignant   mad
nettled   peeved   riled   vexed*

47   **animal**   n.

beast   brute   creature   mammal

48   **annoying**   adj.

bothersome   irritating   troublesome

harassing   very tiring through
  continual worry or bother
nagging   finding fault continually
tormenting   teasing or worrying
  excessively
vexatious   very irritating or worrying

infuriating   maddening   vexing

49   **another**   adj.

*a different   a distinct   a further
an additional   an extra   a separate
a supplementary*

50   **answer**   v. (i)

reply   respond

acknowledge   report that one has
  received something
confirm   establish more firmly the
  truth of; say again to make
  more definite
rejoin   reply
retort   reply quickly, sometimes
  cuttingly, often wittily
riposte   reply quickly and cleverly

get back at   retaliate

51   **answer**   v. (ii)

solve

justify   give or be a good reason for
satisfy   provide with sufficient proof
  to convince

52   **anyhow**   adv. (i)

anyway   by any means   at all events
at any rate   in any case

53   **anyhow**   adv. (ii)

*carelessly   haphazardly   heedlessly
mindlessly   negligently   sloppily*

54   **appear**   v. (i)

emerge

come into view   come up or out
come to light   reveal by investigation
loom   appear close at hand or with
  threatening aspect
rise up   become visible

55 appear v. (ii)

look as if   look like   seem

strike one as being   wear the aspect of

56 approach v.

come close   come near   draw near
move closer to

57 argue v.

dispute

bandy words   exchange remarks in a
  quarrel
cavil   find fault unnecessarily
contend   compete; fight for something
debate   discuss or consider formally
quibble   make petty objections

58 around adv.

*far and wide   here and there
in all directions   in all parts
on all sides   on most sides*

59 artful adj.

crafty   cunning

canny   not easily deceived
foxy   not to be trusted
knowing   showing secret
  understanding
sly   dishonestly tricky

calculating   scheming   shifty

60 ashamed adj.

abashed   feeling ill at ease or confused
embarrassed   feeling awkward
humiliated   disgraced; having lost the
  respect of others

chagrined

61 ask v.

enquire

interrogate   question closely or
  formally
query   express doubts about
question   seek information
quiz   test or examine the knowledge
  of

beg   beseech   request

62 assess v.

judge

consider   think about
evaluate   calculate the value
investigate   examine thoroughly
review   re-examine or survey
weigh up   consider carefully

63 attack v.

assail   attack violently and
  persistently
assault   attack suddenly and violently
  with blows
beseige   surround with armed forces
blitz   attack suddenly and violently,
  especially from the air
bombard   send a barrage of shells
  against; bomb heavily
raid   make a sudden surprise visit to
  catch someone or seize something
storm   capture through using great
  violence, especially a fortress
strafe   spray with bullets from low-
  flying aircraft

64 attitude n.

demeanour   how a person behaves
  towards others
opinion   what one thinks on a
  particular point
outlook   a person's mental attitude or
  way of looking at something

*frame of mind   mental state
temperament*

65 attract v.

allure attract by offering something
 pleasant
charm please; win over; delight
enchant fill with intense delight

enamour

66 auburn adj.

bronze copper golden-brown
henna reddish-brown
russet rust

67 average adj.

ordinary typical

middling neither good nor bad
moderate medium in amount,
 intensity, or rate
normal conforming to what is
 standard
standard generally recognized as
 correct

fair-to-middling run-of-the-mill

68 aware adj.

conscious knowing; understanding
mindful giving thought or careful
 attention to; not forgetful of

alive to conversant informed
observant

69 awful adj. (i)

dreaded dreadful spine-chilling
terrible

70 awful adj. (ii)

distasteful nasty repulsive shoddy
third-rate

71 awkward adj. (i)

cumbersome clumsy to wear or carry
 or manage
ill-adapted altered clumsily and
 unsuitably
unmanageable unable to be
 controlled
unsuitable not fitted for its purpose
unwieldy difficult to move, use, or
 control

inappropriate inconvenient
inopportune untimely

72 awkward adj. (ii)

clumsy

aggressive crude gawky ungainly

73 baby n.

infant newborn

foundling a deserted child of
 unknown parents
toddler child who has recently learnt
 to walk
tot very small child

bairn nursling

74 bad adj.

corrupt accepting bribes; morally
 depraved
dangerous liable to cause harm
dishonest untruthful and
 untrustworthy
evil very bad; harmful; sinful
immoral not considered good or right
unscrupulous not caring about
 honesty or fairness
wicked greatly offending against
 what is right

criminal villainous

75 bag n.

*attaché case   briefcase   carpet bag
carrier   duffle bag   grip
handbag   haversack   holdall
kitbag   pouch   purse   rucksack
sack   satchel   suitcase*

76 baggy adj.

loose   puffy   shapeless   slack

77 banish v.

exile   send away

expel   force to leave school or country
ostracize   refuse to have social
  dealings with
outlaw   declare to have lost the
  protection given by law

78 bar v. (i)

bolt   fasten   lock   lock up   secure

79 bar v. (ii)

ban   forbid officially
boycott   refuse to have anything to do
  with
impede   make difficult to act or go
  forward
prohibit   forbid

blacklist   exclude   hinder

80 bay n.

basin   deep part of a harbour; wide
  part of a canal
bight   long inward curve in a coast
cove   small, sheltered opening in the
  coastline
creek   narrow, long inlet of water
  from sea or lake into the land
estuary   mouth of large river into
  which sea enters at high tide

fiord   deep, narrow arm of sea
  between cliffs, especially in Norway
gulf   area of sea partly surrounded by
  land, larger than a bay
harbour   place of shelter for ships
inlet   strip of water extending into the
  land from sea or lake, or between
  islands
mouth   place where a river enters the
  sea

81 become v.

*change into   come to be   develop into
evolve into   grow into   mature into
pass into   ripen into   turn into*

82 bed n.

bunk   narrow bed fixed to the wall
cot   child's bed with high sides
cradle   small bed for a baby, usually
  on rockers
crib   baby's cot
hammock   hanging bed of canvas or
  rope network
palliasse   straw mattress
recliner   armchair whose back can be
  lowered for sleeping on

83 beer n.

ale   pale-coloured beer
bitter   beer strongly flavoured with
  hops
lager   light gassy beer
mild   beer not strongly flavoured
stout   strong, dark beer

84 before adv.

*earlier   formerly   in the past
previously*

85 begin v.

commence   start

embark   begin an undertaking
establish   set up on a permanent basis
found   start a company or
  organization
inaugurate   begin officially or
  formally; open with a ceremony
initiate   start a scheme working;
  introduce, especially with a ceremony
instigate   start something happening
  by one's own action
launch   send off; start a project
pioneer   take part in a course of
  action that leads the way for others
  to follow

set in motion

86 begrudge v.

be jealous of   feel or show resentment
envy   feel discontent at another's
  qualities or possessions
resent   feel angry or bitter at

87 belief n.

acceptance   willingness to agree to
assent   agreement with an idea
assurance   strong faith in one's own
  ability; trustworthy statement
certainty   freedom from doubt;
  established fact
confidence   firm trust
faith   complete trust in a person or
  thing
reliance   confidence felt about
  something
trust   firm belief in the honesty,
  worth, or power of someone or
  something

88 believe v.

acknowledge   admit; recognize the
  existence of

assert   state forcefully
assume   take as true without proof;
  suppose
conclude   arrive at a belief or opinion
  by reasoning
consider   think about, especially so as
  to make a decision
deduce   decide from general principles
maintain   assert as true
recognize   acknowledge formally as
  being genuine

postulate

89 belongings n.

effects   personal effects   possessions

article   particular thing or object
gear   set of things collected together
  for a particular purpose
goods   movable property; articles of
  trade
kit   clothing and personal equipment
  of a soldier, sailor, traveller,
  or sportsperson
luggage   cases and bags of a traveller
property   thing or things owned

equipment

90 bend v.

contort   twist severely out of shape
curve   bend round with no sharp
  angles
flex   move so as to stretch and loosen
twist   move in a winding course
meander   follow a winding course

coil   loop   zigzag

91 beside prep.

alongside   by   by the side of
close by   near to   next to
on the edge of   not relevant to

92 besides adv.

*furthermore   moreover
on top of everything else*

93 besides prep.

apart from   except for   in addition

94 betray v.
break faith with

give away   inform against

95 beware v.

*be alert   be careful   be wary
guard against   take heed   watch out*

96 beyond prep.

*across   further on   in excess of
on the farther side of
on the other side of   out of reach of*

97 big adj.
large

*colossal   elephantine   enormous
gargantuan   gigantic   huge
immense   vast*

98 billowy adj.

*heaving   rippling   rolling   surging
tossing   undulating*

99 bit n.
fragment   piece   scrap

morsel   small piece of food
portion   part or share of something
sliver   small, thin, sharp piece cut or
  torn off

mouthful

100 bitter adj. (i)

acid   sharp-tasting; sour-tasting
biting   smarting and unpleasant in the
  mouth
pungent   strong, sharp taste or smell

acrid   astringent

101 bitter adj. (ii)

distressing   causing suffering, sorrow,
  or pain
grievous   seriously harmful; severe
harrowing   causing pain and worry

102 bitter adj. (iii)

acrimonious   sharpness of manner or
  temper
caustic   sarcastic

103 black adj.

coal-black   black as coal
ebony   like the hard, dark wood of a
  tropical tree
pitch-black   completely black, with
  no light at all
raven   glossy black

*besmirched   dingy   grimy   sooty
sullied*

104 blame v.
hold responsible

cast aspersions on   make accusations
  without proof
reproach   express disapproval, not
  angrily but sadly

point the finger at

105 blank adj. (i)

*bare   unadorned   undecorated
unmarked*

106 **blank** adj. (ii)

bewildered puzzled
confused mixed up in thoughts and feelings
expressionless showing nothing in face or voice
poker-faced not revealing thoughts or feelings

107 **blatant** adj.

arrant utter; out-and-out; downright
brazen shameless
flagrant open and shameless
flaunting displaying in an offensive way
glaring very obvious
obtrusive unpleasantly noticeable
offensive insulting; disgusting

108 **bleak** adj.

arid parched and desert-like
cheerless dreary and without comfort
desolate dismal and deserted by people
exhausted used up completely
uncultivable unable to grow crops
unproductive producing little of value

unsheltered windswept

109 **blue** adj. (i)

azure sky-blue
aquamarine. pale blue to greenish-blue colour
lapis lazuli brilliant deep blue
sapphire transparent bright blue
turquoise sky blue or greenish-blue

110 **blue** adj (ii)

despondent downcast unhappy

doleful mournful and dreary in a self-pitying way

glum in low spirits, especially because of disappointment

depressed

111 **boastful** adj.

bragging

arrogant proud and self-important in a rude way
blustering talking aggressively, especially with empty threats
crowing loudly exulting or triumphing
overbearing bossy in manner or action
vaunting bragging; blowing one's own trumpet

112 **boat** n.

craft

canoe long, light narrow boat, pointed at both ends, moved by a paddle
coracle small wicker-basket boat, covered with watertight material
dinghy small open boat for rowing or sailing
dugout boat made by hollowing a tree trunk
galleon large 15th-17th century sailing ship, usually Spanish
galley ancient or medieval warship or trader propelled by oars and/or sails
houseboat barge-like boat fitted up as a dwelling
kayak small, light, covered canoe, first used by Eskimos
launch large motor boat
packet boat for carrying mail, and often people as well
pinnace small boat used by a ship
punt flat-bottomed river boat propelled by a long pole
skiff small light boat for rowing, sculling or sailing

sloop   single-masted sailing vessel, rigged fore-and-aft

tender   boat travelling to and from a larger one to convey stores or passengers

tug   small powerful boat for towing others

yacht   light sailing boat, used either for racing or pleasure cruises

113   bog   n.

mire

fen   low-lying marshy or flooded land

marsh   land that is all or partly soft and wet

morass   stretch of soft, wet ground, dangerous for walking

quagmire   soft, wet area of land that gives way under the feet

swamp   permanently waterlogged ground, usually overgrown

114   bold   adj.

daring   unafraid

plucky   brave and determined

115   bonus   n.

award   given officially as a payment or prize

dividend   share of profits paid to shareholders or winners

fringe benefit   added favours or services given with a job

gratuity   money given in recognition of services rendered; a tip

handout   something distributed free of charge

present   something given or received as a gift

reward

116   book   n.

album   book used for collections, e.g. photographs, stamps

anthology   collection of passages from literature, especially poems

classic   work of literature of lasting importance

diary   daily record of events or thoughts

dictionary   book that lists words in alphabetical order, with their meanings

encyclopaedia   book or set of books dealing with branches of knowledge, usually in alphabetical order

handbook   small book giving useful facts

journal   daily record of news, events, or business dealings

ledger   business account book

log   detailed record of a ship's voyage or an aircraft's flight

manual   book, especially of instructions or information

manuscript   author's work as written or typed

novel   book-length story about imaginary people

paperback   book bound in a flexible paper binding

publication   something printed and issued to the public

romance   imaginative story of love and adventure

textbook   book for studying a particular subject

thesaurus   dictionary of words arranged according to likenesses in their meaning

thriller   exciting story

tome   large, heavy book

tract   pamphlet on a moral or religious subject

treatise   written work dealing systematically with one subject

volume   one of a set of books of the same kind

117 boost v.

advance   help the progress of
advertise   make thing known publicly, especially to encourage people to buy
advocate   speak in favour of
back   support and encourage, often with money
facilitate   ease the path of
further   help the progress of
promote   help forward
publicize   bring to the attention of the public

recommend

118 boring adj.

humdrum   without change; dull and commonplace
irksome   causing vexation, annoyance, or boredom
monotonous   lacking variety
repetitious   containing things said or done many times
tedious   tiresome because of its length, slowness or dullness
unvaried   unchanging

tiresome

119 boundary n.

limit

border   edge; dividing line between two countries
circumference   distance round a circle or circular area
frontier   line where two countries meet
perimeter   outer edge of an area
periphery   outside edge of an area; outer or surrounding region of area

bounds

120 box n.

bin   large, rigid container with lid
cabinet   piece of furniture with drawers and shelves
caddy   small box or tin for holding tea
carton   box made from cardboard for holding goods

casket   small, usually ornamental, box for holding valuables
chest   large, strong box for storing or shipping things
coffer   large, strong box for holding money and valuables
container   box, barrel, or bottle for holding something
crate   packing-case made of wooden slats
locker   small cupboard or compartment where things can be stowed safely
receptacle   something for holding or containing what is put into it
safe   box or cupboard with thick metal sides and lock, used to store valuables
strong-box   strongly-made small chest for valuables
trunk   large box with hinged lid for transporting or storing clothes

121 boy n.

lad

adolescent   young person between about 13 and 16
child   young person below the age of puberty
juvenile   young person
minor   person not yet reached the age at which he is fully responsible in law for his actions
stripling   young man
teenager   person aged between 13 and 19
urchin   mischievous or needy child
youngster   young person; child or youth
youth   person between childhood and maturity

122 brave adj.

courageous   fearless   valiant

dauntless   not discouraged or afraid
gallant   honourable and high spirited
heroic   quite exceptionally brave
intrepid   daring and without fear

chivalrous

123 break v.

chip cut or break a small piece from the surface or edge
crack break without dividing into separate parts
crash have or cause to have a sudden violent and noisy accident
crush press so as to break, injure, or wrinkle; squeeze tightly
fracture break or crack, especially of a bone
grind crush into grains or powder by pressing between hard surfaces
shatter break suddenly and violently into small pieces
smash break or become broken suddenly and noisily into pieces
snap suddenly break off
splinter break into needle-like pieces
split divide along a length, especially with force

124 breathe v.

exhale breathe out
gasp catch the breath suddenly and audibly
inhale breathe in deeply
pant breathe with short, quick breaths
puff breathe rapidly and with effort
wheeze make a noisy whistling sound when breathing

respire

125 bright adj. (i)

glossy shiny and smooth
glowing giving out light and heat without flame
incandescent giving a bright light when heated
luminous giving out light; glowing in the dark
radiant giving out rays of light
shiny rubbed until bright

126 bright adj. (ii)

animated full of life and excitement
cheerful in good spirits
gay light-hearted and full of fun
lively full of life

127 brilliant adj.

blinding too bright to see clearly
dazzling bright and confusing
scintillating twinkling very brightly
sparkling shining brightly in small flashes
vivid intense, bright and clear

128 bring v.

cause make happen
conduct guide or lead
escort accompany someone
lead show the way

129 brunette adj.

brown-haired

130 brutal adj.

callous without feelings; hardened
inhumane not showing normal qualities of kindness, pity, or sympathy

vicious *merciless*

131 build v.

construct

erect *put up*

132 bungle v.

botch spoil or repair badly by lack of skill or care
mismanage handle badly or wrongly

133 busy adj.

absorbed   active   engaged
occupied   working

134 busybody n.

backbiter   person who talks spitefully
about others in their absence
eavesdropper   person who listens
secretly to a conversation
gossip   person who talks casually
about other people's lives
meddler   person who interferes in
other people's affairs
muckraker   person who seeks and
tells unpleasant stories about
others
newsmonger   someone who enjoys
gossiping
slanderer   someone who deliberately
spreads false reports about others
snooper   someone who pries into the
private business of others
tale-bearer   someone who nastily
spreads unkind or false stories
about others

135 but conj. and prep.

except   nevertheless   on the contrary
on the other hand   save   yet

136 calm adj. (i)

peaceful   quiet   still

placid   having a calm appearance or
nature
serene   completely calm and peaceful
tranquil   undisturbed; not agitated

becalmed   undisturbed

137 calm adj. (ii)

collected   composed

imperturbable   unable to be worried
or excited

serene   unable to be troubled or
agitated

cool   cool-headed   even-tempered
self-controlled   self-possessed

138 car n.

automobile   motorcar

convertible   car with a roof that can
be folded down or removed
coupé   closed two-door car with a
sloping back
hatchback   car with a sloping back
hinged at the top so that it can
be opened
hearse   vehicle for carrying the coffin
at a funeral
jalopy   battered old car
jeep   small sturdy motor vehicle with
four-wheel drive
limousine   large luxurious car, usually
with glass between driver and
passengers
roadster   open car, especially with
two seats
saloon   car with roof, closed sides,
windows, and a separate boot
sports car   open, low-built fast car
taxi   car with its driver hired by the
public

139 care n.

anxiety   trouble   worry

apprehension   feeling of fear or
anxiety about a possible danger
or difficulty
concern   serious care for or interest in
misgiving   feeling of doubt or slight
fear or mistrust
uneasiness   mental or physical
discomfort

grief   sorrow

140 careful adj.

cautious very watchful
chary cautious; wary
concerned giving time or attention to
conscientious showing or done with
serious attention
meticulous giving great attention to
detail; very exact
painstaking taking great care
protective wanting to keep from
harm or injury
wary looking out for possible danger
or difficulty

fastidious finicky hesitant

141 careless adj.

inattentive negligent thoughtless

neglectful leaving undone; not giving
due care to
remiss neglecting duty
unheeding deliberately not listening
or paying attention
unorganized unplanned and
disorderly

blasé happy-go-lucky

142 careworn adj.

*bowed down dispirited exhausted
haggard*

143 carry v.

bear

cart carry with great labour
convey take or carry from one place
to another
deliver take to the intended person or
place
drag pull along with effort or
difficulty
haul pull or drag forcibly; transport
by a truck
lug carry or drag with great effort

support hold in position; bear the
weight of
transmit send or pass from one
person, place, or thing to another
transport take from place to place

144 case n.

matter

affair concern or business
circumstance manner, time, place of
an act or event; detail or fact
event thing that happens, especially
of importance
instance example; particular case
situation place; position

plight problem

145 casual adj. (i)

fortuitous happening by a lucky
chance
nonchalant casually unconcerned or
not interested
offhand short and disrespectful in
speech and manner
unexpected happening without being
previously thought of

casual adj. (ii)

informal without ceremony

146 catch v.

capture

arrest seize someone by authority of
the law
grab seize something or someone
with a sudden rough movement
net catch in, or as if in, a net
snare catch in, or as if in, a noose

take into custody

147 catching adj.

contagious able to be spread by touch or closeness
infectious able to be spread by air or water

transferrable transmissible

148 cause n.

reason

agent person or thing that produces an effect, change, or result
creator one who brings something into existence
inducement encouragement to do something
inspiration something or someone that rouses the mind and feelings to special activity
motive reason for action
originator person who begins or causes the beginning of something
source person or thing that supplies information; starting point
stimulus something that causes activity

explanation

149 celebrate v.

acclaim salute with cheering and clapping
commemorate honour or keep alive the memory of
extol praise very highly
observe follow a custom, tradition, law, or holiday
pay homage carry out a ceremony to honour someone

150 celebrated adj.

famous renowned

eminent very well-known and admired; outstanding

prominent important and well-known
respected very well thought of

acclaimed venerable

151 chair n.

armchair chair with raised sides or arms
deckchair portable folding chair of canvas on wood or metal frame
easy chair big comfortable chair, usually with arms
rocking chair chair on curved supports that can be moved gently backwards and forwards
seat anything that can be sat on
settee seat for two or more, with back and usually arms, part of a three-piece suite
throne special chair used by a king, queen, or bishop on ceremonial occasions
wheelchair invalid's chair on wheels

152 change v.

alter

convert change from one substance, state, use, or purpose to another
interchange put each of two things into the other's place
modify make slight changes
replace find or provide a substitute for
transform change completely in appearance or nature

recast restyle

153 changeable adj.

variable

chequered marked by frequent changes of good and bad luck

fickle   not constant or loyal in love or
  friendship
inconstant   changeable and unfaithful
  in feeling
indecisive   not firm or steady in
  purpose or action
unreliable   not able to be trusted
unstable   tending to change suddenly
  in feelings or behaviour

154   chaos   n.

confusion   disorder

bedlam   scene of wild, noisy activity
rumpus   loud and angry dispute
turmoil   state of great confusion,
  excitement, and trouble
upheaval   great change and
  movement
upset   disturbance of normal course
  of events

155   character   n.

ego   favourable image of oneself
individuality   qualities that make one
  person different from another
nature   fundamental qualities of a
  person or thing

attribute   idiosyncrasy   trait

156   charming   adj.

appealing   able to arouse pleasurable
  feelings
attractive   pleasing in appearance or
  effect
delightful   highly pleasing
engaging   occupying the pleased
  attention of
winning   persuasive
winsome   sweetly charming in
  manner and appearance

*alluring   beguiling   captivating
enchanting   enticing   entrancing
irresistible*

157   chase   v.

pursue   run after

hunt   pursue for food or sport, or
  with hostility
run down   chase and overtake animal
  or person
shadow   follow and watch secretly
stalk   follow or approach game
  stealthily and quietly
track   find and follow marks left by a
  moving person, animal or thing
trail   follow marks left by person or
  animal

158   cheap   adj.

inexpensive   low-priced

bargain   very cheap
economical   avoiding waste
reasonable   fair; not expensive
reduced   lowered in price

159   cheat   v.

deceive   trick

delude   mislead or trick
fleece   charge far too much, or
  defraud
rook   swindle; charge far too high a
  price
swindle   obtain by fraud

160   cheek   n.

impudence   insolence   pertness

audacity   bold and reckless
  impudence

161   cheer   v. (i)

applaud   clap

cheer   v. (ii)

gladden   comfort

162 **cheerful** adj.

cheery   in good spirits

amiable   feeling and inspiring
  friendliness; good-tempered
jovial   full of cheerful good humour
joyful   full of happiness
merry   laughingly cheerful
optimistic   believing things will turn
  out well
vivacious   high-spirited

light-hearted

163 **cheering** adj.

heartening

auspicious   giving signs of future
  success
stimulating   making more vigorous or
  active

comforting   encouraging   reassuring

164 **cheerless** adj.

dreary   gloomy

dingy   dirty and faded
dismal   causing gloom and depression
drab   monotonous; dull
murky   dark and unpleasant
sombre   full of shadows

abandoned   depressing   uninviting

165 **chiefly** adv.

especially   mainly   predominantly
principally

essentially   most importantly;
  necessarily
particularly   for one definite or
  particular point

above all   first and foremost

166 **choke** v.

asphyxiate   make or become unable
  to breathe
block   obstruct
clog   make or become filled with thick
  or sticky matter
obstruct   place something to prevent
  or hinder movement or progress
smother   die or kill through lack of air
stifle   feel, or cause to feel, unable to
  breathe
strangle   kill by squeezing neck;
  throttle
suffocate   kill, or be killed, by lack of
  oxygen

garrotte   throttle

167 **choose** v.

pick   select

adopt   take and use as one's own
cull   select from flock and kill,
  especially surplus animals
elect   choose by vote
opt for   show preference for
prefer   like better
single out   separate from others for
  special treatment or notice

favour

168 **chronic** adj.

*continual   deep-rooted   ingrained
long-standing   persistent*

169 **civil** adj.

mannerly   polite

agreeable   to one's liking
courteous   polite and considerate in
  manner
deferential   showing polite respect
formal   correct in manner and
  behaviour
respectful   feeling or showing
  consideration or admiration

170 class n.

category   division   group

branch   subdivision
set   group of naturally connected
  things

171 claw v.

gouge   scoop or force out
lacerate   injure by tearing jaggedly
rend   tear with violent force
rip   tear quickly and violently
tear   pull apart or into pieces by force

172 clean adj.

spotless   unsoiled

laundered   washed and pressed
scoured   cleaned by hard rubbing
  with a rough material
uncorrupted   moral; free from
  dishonesty and wickedness
unstained   without being discoloured
  or darkened in any way
untainted   without trace of decay or
  infection

173 clear adj. (i)

transparent

limpid   clear, calm and peaceful
translucent   allowing some light to
  pass through

174 clear adj. (ii)

bright   cloudless   sunny

175 clever adj.

brainy   intelligent   sharp-witted

accomplished   able to do many things
brilliant   outstandingly clever
gifted   having great natural ability

ingenious   clever at inventing new
  things or methods
inventive   able to invent or think in
  new ways
precocious   showing unusually early
  development of mind or body
resourceful   able to get round
  difficulties
sharp   quick to see, hear, or notice
  things
skilful   able to do something well and
  easily
smart   good or quick in thinking or
  speaking
talented   having very great natural
  ability or aptitude

176 climb v.

ascend   scale

clamber   climb with some difficulty,
  using both feet and hands
mount   get up on
scramble up   move hastily and
  awkwardly up a rough, steep slope

creep up   trail up   twine up

177 close v.

shut

close off   put up a barrier
close up   shut up completely
seal   close securely to prevent entry
seal off   close tightly to prevent
  escape or entry

barricade   blockade

178 close adj.(i)

compact   closely or neatly packed
  together
dense   massed closely together
stuffy   lacking sufficient fresh air

airless

close adj.(ii)

secretive hiding one's intentions or
plans

179 **clutter** n.

hotch-potch things mixed up without
any order
huddle confused mass of people or
things
jumble muddle; confused collection
of things
litter odds and ends of rubbish left
lying about
lumber useless or unwanted articles
stored away
mess untidy collection of things

180 **coat** n.

anorak short coat with hood to keep
out wind, rain, and cold
duffle coat loose coat of heavy cloth,
fastened with toggles
greatcoat heavy overcoat, especially
military
jerkin sleeveless jacket
parka jacket with hood, with fur
inside
tunic close-fitting jacket worn as part
of a uniform
windcheater sports jacket of thin but
windproof material, fitting closely
at waist and cuffs

blazer jacket mackintosh
overcoat raincoat sports jacket

181 **coax** v.

persuade

beguile win the attention or interest
of; amuse
cajole persuade by flattery or
pleasing talk
entreat beg earnestly or emotionally
flatter praise too much or insincerely
in order to please someone

wheedle persuade by flattery or
endearments; get something out
of someone
wile lure, beguile, or entice

182 **code** n.

criterion standard of judgement
guideline principle by which to set
standards or determine actions
law rule supported by government
power that members of society must
follow
morals rules of behaviour based on
people's sense of what is right or just
principles high personal standards of
what is right and wrong
rules orders that guide actions or
describe events

183 **cold** adj.

bitter piercingly cold
chilly unpleasantly cold
freezing cold enough for water to
turn to ice
frigid intensely cold
glacial extremely cold, reminding one
of a glacier
icy as cold as ice
sharp keen and biting
sunless without sunshine

184 **collect** v.

accumulate gather

amass gather in great amounts
assemble fit, put, or gather together
compile collect or arrange into a list
or book
garner collect and store up
glean gather scraps of information;
pick up grain left after harvesters
harvest gather a crop
muster gather together troops for
inspection or duty

flock together store up stow away

185 colour v.

brighten add fresh colour
daub coat or smear roughly
dye stain; make something a
  specified colour
paint apply colour, especially with
  brush
shade darken so as to give the effect
  of light and shadow
tincture add a slight trace of colour
tinge change the colour slightly
tint apply or give a slight colour to

186 come v.

approach come nearer
arrive come to destination
reach go as far as

move towards

187 comfort v.

console

reassure remove fear or doubt
relieve make something less
  unpleasant, hard, or monotonous
solace comfort or cheer in distress
support help with sympathy,
  practical advice, or money

encourage

188 comfortable adj.

*at ease at rest cosy homelike
relaxed*

189 compare v.

contrast show clearly the differences
  between two things
correlate compare and connect
  systematically
differentiate recognize as different
examine look at closely to find out
  something

judge give a decision or opinion
  about
liken point out the resemblance of
  one thing to another
measure estimate by comparing with
  some standard

190 complacent adj.

pleased with oneself   self-contented
self-satisfied

smug far too self-satisfied

191 concerning prep.

about   regarding   relating to

*referring to   respecting
with reference to*

192 condemn v.

censure express strong criticism or
  disapproval
convict prove or declare a person to
  be guilty of a crime
denounce speak publicly against;
  give information against
sentence give punishment from a
  court of law

193 confirm v.

verify

affirm state as a fact
bear witness to provide evidence of
  the truth
clinch settle something in a definite
  way, such as an argument or a deal
corroborate confirm formally,
  especially in law
sanction give approval to; authorize

194 confused adj.

bewildered   mixed up

baffled puzzled

muddled   mixed up mentally

all at sea   *at a loss*   *in a stupor*
mystified   *non-plussed*   *perplexed*

195   consult   v.
seek advice from

confer with   discuss; consult together

seek information from   *seek the
opinion of*

196   contact   v.

approach   *communicate with*
get in touch with   *look up*   *notify*

197   container   n.
receptacle

hamper   large basket with a lid
hopper   funnel through which grain
 or coal is passed
repository   place where things are
 stored
reservoir   place where liquid is stored,
 especially water for a city
vessel   receptacle for holding liquids

basin   *basket*   *bin*   *bottle*   *bowl*
box   *dustbin*   *jar*

198   contempt   n.
disdain

disrespect   rudeness
loathing   great hatred or disgust
scorn   open ridicule

disgust   *revulsion*

199   continual   adj.

frequent   *recurrent*   *repeated*

200   continuous   adj.

connected   *constant*   *incessant*
perpetual   *unbroken*   *uninterrupted*

201   convenient   adj.

handy   *nearby*   *useful*   *within reach*

202   cook   v.

barbecue   cook over an open fire on a
 metal frame
braise   cook slowly in a covered dish
broil   cook meat on a fire or gridiron
sauté   fry quickly in a little hot oil or
 fat
simmer   boil very gently
steam   cook above boiling water

roast

203   copy   n.
replica

carbon   exact copy made with carbon
 paper
counterfeit   close copy made in order
 to deceive
duplicate   one of two or more things
 that are exactly alike
forgery   exact copy made in order to
 defraud
imitation   something made to appear
 like something else
likeness   sameness in form;
 resemblance
semblance   outward appearance of,
 either real or pretended; a show

204   correct   adj.
accurate   right

factual   based on or containing facts
faithful   true to the facts or to an
 original
literal   following the usual meaning of
 the words

precise exact; correctly and clearly
  stated
unerring without making a mistake

205 corrupt adj.

immoral

deceitful not telling the truth
depraved having a bad character
dishonourable shameful
immoral lacking in, or not
  conforming to, accepted principles
  of what is right and wrong
perverted the opposite of what is
  regarded as normal or right
tainted infected with disease; moral
  decay
untrustworthy unreliable;
  undependable

bribable *degenerate*

206 crash n.

collapse *collision* *smash-up*

207 creep v.

crawl inch along move stealthily

208 cringe v.

cower bend down, especially in fear
fawn upon try to gain favour by
  over-praising and insincere attention
flinch draw back; wince
grovel be shamefully humble and
  eager to please
quail lose courage; give way before
recoil draw back suddenly in fear or
  disgust
shrink draw into oneself; cower

209 crisp adj.

abrupt sudden and unexpected;
  rough and impolite

brisk quick and active
concise brief, giving much
  information in few words
decisive showing firmness in settling
  something quickly

210 crockery n.

china collective name for thin, fine
  crockery
earthenware pots made of coarse
  baked clay
porcelain finest kind of china, thin
  and shiny
pottery handmade pots and other
  objects
stoneware heavy pottery made from
  clay containing flint
terracotta brownish-red unglazed
  pottery

211 crowd n.

throng

company number of guests: people
  combined together for business or
  trade
horde vast crowd
host large number of people or things
mob large, disorderly crowd of
  people
multitude very great number of
  things or people

audience *body* *gang* *group*
rabble

212 cruel adj.

bloodthirsty eager for bloodshed
brutal merciless; very cruel
inhuman lacking normal human
  qualities of kindness, pity, sympathy
  and understanding
pitiless showing no tender human
  feeling
remorseless showing no sorrow for
  having done wrong

sadistic   enjoying inflicting or
  watching cruelty
vicious   morally evil; having a desire
  to hurt

implacable

213   cry   v.

shed tears   weep

blubber   weep noisily
mourn   grieve for a person who has
  died or for a thing lost
sob   draw breath heavily and noisily
  while weeping
wail   utter a long cry of grief or pain
whimper   make feeble, frightened or
  complaining sounds
whine   complain in a petty or feeble
  way

214   cunning   adj.

artful   crafty   foxy   sly   wily

guileful   full of deceitful tricks
scheming   planning in a secret and
  underhand way
shrewd   clever in judging what is to
  one's advantage

shifty   *tricky*   *underhand*

215   cut   v.

carve   cut in order to make a special
  shape; cut up meat
cleave   divide by chopping; split
  along natural lines
dissect   cut into parts in order to
  study
gash   make a long, deep wound
slash   cut with long forceful strokes
  with a knife, sword, or whip
slice   cut cleanly into thin, flat pieces
slit   make a narrow cut or opening

disjoint   *section*   *sever*   *sunder*

216   daft   adj.

addle-pated   *crack-brained*   *crazy*
feather-brained   *half-baked*
mad as a hatter   *not all there*
senseless   *weak-minded*

217   damp   adj.

moist

clammy   unpleasantly moist and
  sticky
dank   unpleasantly cold and damp
humid   damp air or climate
misty   indistinct because of water
  vapour in the air
muggy   unpleasantly warm and damp

drizzly   *steamy*

218   danger   n.

peril

hazard   exposure to injury, loss, or
  evil
jeopardy   danger of injury, loss, or
  death
menace   threat of harm
risk   possibility of meeting danger,
  suffering harm or loss
threat   indication of something
  harmful or undesirable

219   dark   adj.

dreary   dull, sad and monotonous
funereal   dark and mournful
gloomy   almost dark; unlighted

220   dated   adj.

out-of-date

obsolescent   going out of use or
  fashion
obsolete   no longer used
old-fashioned   of a type no longer in
  style
passé   past its, or his or her, prime

221 dawn n. (i)

daybreak

cockcrow   crack-of-dawn
early light   sunrise

222 dawn n. (ii)

beginning

advent   coming of one who is awaited
arrival   appearance of
emergence   coming up, or out, or into
  view
inception   beginning of the existence
  of something

awakening   birth   foundation

223 dazzle v.

blind   take away the power of
  judgement
daze   make unable to think or feel
  clearly
overawe   fill with wonder and fear
stagger   cause astonishment, worry,
  or confusion
stun   shock into helplessness

amaze   baffle   bewilder   disconcert
dumbfound   nonplus   strike dumb

224 dazzling adj.

overpowering   extremely intense
resplendent   gloriously bright and
  shiny

blinding   brilliant

225 dead adj. (i)

deceased   lifeless

defunct   no longer existing or
  functioning
departed   sympathetic word for the
  dead

extinct   no longer existing in living
  form
inanimate   showing no sign of life
perished   having met a violent or
  untimely death

226 dead adj. (ii)

dead centre   dead end   dead level
dead silence

227 dear adj.

costly   expensive   highly-priced

228 deathless adj.

immortal   imperishable   undying

eternal   existing always without
  beginning or end
everlasting   never coming to an end
timeless   independent of time
unending   continuing for ever

historic

229 deceit n.

deception

dissimulation   concealment of one's
  feelings and intentions
duplicity   trickery by dishonest
  behaviour and dealing
fraud   dishonest trick for the purpose
  of gain
hoax   deceiving by way of a joke
swindle   cheating in a business deal

double-dealing

230 decent adj.

respectable

befitting   right and suitable
proper   paying great attention to
  what is considered correct in society

obliging

231 decide v.

determine

adjudicate judge and pronounce a
  decision upon
arbitrate settle a dispute without bias
settle decide on, fix, or arrange

form an opinion *referee*

232 decoration n.

adornment ornament; something
  adding beauty to
embellishment improvement by
  adding detail or ornament
ornament decorative object or detail

frill *nick-nack* *trinket*

233 defeat v.

beat

conquer overcome by force or effort
crush defeat and control completely
overrun spread over and occupy;
  devastate
overthrow remove from power;
  defeat
overwhelm overcome by force
  completely and suddenly
rout put to flight
subdue bring under control
vanquish defeat in a battle or contest

get the better of *thrash* *trounce*

234 defend v.

protect

safeguard protect from danger,
  damage, or injury
shield hide from harm or danger

speak up for *stand up for*

235 define v.

explain exactly   outline clearly

characterize describe the essential
  qualities of
elucidate make clear; throw light on
  a problem

lay down *set out*

236 defy v.

resist openly

challenge dare; threaten
confront face boldly or threateningly
deride laugh at scornfully
disobey not obey; go against
  someone's will or command
disregard pay no attention to; treat
  as of no importance
flout show contempt for

fly in the face of *scoff at*

237 delay v.

put off   postpone

defer put off until later
detain keep waiting; cause delay to
hinder make it difficult for someone
  to do something
impede get in the way of
linger be slow in going
shelve put aside temporarily
suspend put off for a period

lag *slow up*

238 delicious adj.

delectable highly enjoyable,
  especially to the taste
succulent juicy
toothsome of appetizing appearance,
  flavour or smell

appetizing *tasty*

239 deny v.

disclaim say that one does not own or have any connection with
disprove show to be false or wrong
refute prove that a statement, opinion, or person is wrong
reject refuse to accept
repudiate refuse to acknowledge

disown   go without

240 deserve v.

merit   be worthy of

be entitled to   be qualified for
have a claim to   have a right to

241 destroy v.

wreck

demolish pull or knock down
devastate lay waste; cause great destruction to
gut remove or destroy the inside of a building
pulverize crush into powder
ravage do great damage to
wipe out destroy all of something

242 disgraceful adj.

shameful

contemptible deserving to be despised as worthless or bad
odious very offensive
sordid dirty and foul; not honourable

debased   repugnant   shocking

243 do v.

accomplish succeed in doing
achieve finish successfully; gain or reach by effort
act do what is required
develop bring to a later and more advanced stage; grow or cause to grow

discharge carry out a duty, promise, or contract
execute carry out an order or action; put a plan into effect
perform carry out a piece of work or an activity

244 doctor n.

consultant person qualified to give expert medical advice
general practitioner family doctor
physician specialist in medicine as distinct from a surgeon or family doctor
specialist person who is an expert in a special branch of medicine
surgeon doctor whose job is to perform medical operations

homeopath   osteopath

245 dodge v.

avoid

duck lower oneself quickly to avoid being seen or hit
sidestep avoid by stepping sideways
veer change direction or course

dart aside   give the slip   shy away

246 drink v.

carouse have a merry drinking spree
gulp swallow drink or food hastily
guzzle drink or eat greedily
imbibe drink any form of alcohol
quaff drink heartily or in one long draught
swig swallow large mouthfuls
swill drink in large quantities
tipple be in the habit of drinking wine or spirits
toast honour or offer good wishes to someone by drinking

knock back   put away   sip

247 droop v.

sag

flag   become weak and less alive or active
languish   lose or lack will or strength; live under miserable conditions
slouch   stand, sit, or move in a tired-looking, round-shouldered way
slump   sit or flop down heavily and slackly
wilt   become limp from exhaustion or heat

stoop

248 due adj.

expected   owing   payable   rightful

249 dull adj.

boring   uninteresting

insipid   lacking in interest or liveliness
monotonous   lacking variety

dry as dust

250 each adj.

apiece   for everyone   individually
per   to everyone

251 eagerly adv.

enthusiastically   keenly

ardently   full of strong, warm feeling
avidly   greedily; wanting strongly
vehemently   showing a strong, intense feeling
zealously   full of hearty and persistent effort

heartily

252 easily adv.

effortlessly

by far   probably   undoubtedly

253 eat v.

chew   crush or grind with the teeth
devour   eat quickly with great hunger, or like a beast
dine   eat dinner; entertain to dinner
gorge   stuff oneself with food
masticate   chew food
munch   chew steadily and vigorously
nibble   take small, quick or gentle bites

bolt   feast   glut   gobble up
gulp down   tuck in   wolf

254 edge n.

border   boundary or frontier
boundary   limiting or dividing line between surfaces or spaces
brink   edge of a steep place or of a stretch of water
circumference   distance round an object or a place
fringe   edge of an area or group
margin   area on the outside edge of a larger area
perimeter   outer edge of any area
periphery   outside edge of an area; outer or surrounding region of area
verge   extreme edge

extremity   limit   rim   side

255 effect n.

outcome   result

aftermath   what follows after a bad event such as an accident
consequence   result of
issue   outcome; point in question
sequel   what follows or arises out of an earlier event
upshot   final result

256 efficient adj.

adept   highly skilled

capable having the ability to do
something satisfactorily
competent having sufficient skill or
knowledge; capable
expert having great knowledge or
skill
trained able and accustomed to do
something through being taught

masterly

257 effort n.

application careful and continuous
attention or effort
grind hard, uninteresting work
striving struggle towards something
struggle vigorous effort; hard contest
toil long work needing great effort

exertion trouble

258 elsewhere adv.

somewhere else

absent away not here not present

259 emphasize v.

stress

belabour talk about at unnecessary
length
bring home convince
dramatize present in a striking or
exciting manner
feature give special prominence to
highlight draw special attention to
mark notice; watch carefully
underline state forcibly; reinforce

rub in

260 empty adj.

unfurnished unsupplied with what is
necessary for some purpose
unoccupied without anyone or
anything in it

vacant not filled or being used

barren bereft of

261 end n. (i)

close conclusion finish

expiration end of a period of time
finale final section of a musical
composition or a drama
terminus last stop on a railway or bus
route

extremity termination winding-up

262 end n. (ii)

purpose thing intended; object to be
attained

aim goal object objective

263 enemy n.

foe

adversary person or group one is
opposed to
antagonist one who is actively hostile
or opposed to someone or something
assailant person who attacks
another, either by actions or words
attacker person who starts a fight
opponent person who takes the
opposite side

264 energy n.

vigour

drive strong urge and will to do
things
effectiveness ability or power to do
what is necessary
stamina staying-power; ability to
withstand prolonged physical or
mental strain
virility masculine vigour, strength
and power
vitality liveliness; ability to endure

elbow grease

265 engine n.

dynamo small machine turning mechanical energy into electricity
generator apparatus for converting mechanical energy into electrical energy, or for producing a gas
machine man-made instrument for applying mechanical power
motor machine that changes power into movement
transformer apparatus for changing electrical voltage
turbine machine or motor that is driven by a wheel that is itself turned by a flow of water or gas

266 enjoyable adj.

amusing   delightful   diverting
entertaining   pleasurable   satisfying

267 enough adj.

adequate   sufficient

ample more than enough

268 escape v.

get away

abscond go away suddenly and secretly, especially after wrongdoing
elude escape skilfully or by means of a trick
evade avoid by cleverness or trickery

flee

269 essential adj.

indispensable   necessary   vital

basic   fundamental

270 even adj.

flat   level

consistent unchanging; having a regular pattern or style
equable free from extremes; uniform
unvaried staying the same

unchanging

271 event n.

affair   happening   incident
occasion   occurrence

272 evidently adv.

as far as one can see   clearly
obviously   plainly   seemingly

273 examine v.

inspect

analyse separate into parts to find out about
cross-question question closely to test answers to previous questions
probe search into or question closely
scrutinize look at in minute detail
sound out try to find out the opinion or intention of

test

274 example n.

exemplar model; person or thing to be imitated
pattern excellent example to be followed
sample typical small quantity
specimen single typical thing, especially one chosen for showing or testing
standard level of quality considered acceptable

illustration   instance   precedent

275 except prep.

apart from   barring   but   excluding
not counting   omitting

276 excess n.

surfeit

abundance plentiful supply
glut larger supply or quantity than
can be used
surplus amount additional to what is
needed or used; what is left over

plethora superabundance

277 exchange v.

barter trade by exchanging goods for
other goods, not for money
interchange give and receive one
thing for another
substitute put or use one thing
instead of another
swap trade one small thing for
another
trade buy, sell, or exchange

278 exciting adj.

*fascinating irresistible mind-
boggling rousing startling*

279 expect v.

anticipate regard as likely to happen
count on depend on; rely on
foresee be aware of or realize a thing
beforehand

await

280 experienced adj.

practised

competent able to do what is needed
proficient doing something correctly
and satisfactorily through training
or practice
qualified having the abilities,
qualities and skills necessary to do a
particular job

well-grounded

281 explain v.

make plain

clarify make more easily understood
define state or explain the meaning
precisely
expound set forth or explain in detail
interpret understand or show the
meaning of
unfold make clear step by step

account for clear up spell out

282 explore v.

prospect explore in search of
something, such as gold or oil
reconnoitre make a preliminary
survey, usually of an enemy's
position
survey look at and take a general
view of

283 fabulous adj.

*amazing astounding extraordinary
fantastic inconceivable marvellous
miraculous unbelievable wonderful*

284 face n.

countenance expression of the face
expression look that shows one's
feelings
features any of the named parts of
the face
lineaments facial outline or
distinctive characteristic
physiognomy features or expressions
considered as showing personality
visage appearance and aspect of the
face

285 fact n.

detail factor item point truth

286 fade v.

blanch become pale or white
bleach whiten by sunlight or
chemicals
dim become indistinct and not clearly
seen
disappear cease to be visible

cloud *decrease* *grow dull*

287 faint adj. (i)

dim *faded* *indistinct* *obscure*
vague

288 faint adj. (ii)

dizzy *exhausted* *faint-hearted*
giddy

289 fair adj.

just unbiased unprejudiced

detached not influenced by feelings
or other people's opinions
disinterested acting fairly because not
influenced by personal advantage
dispassionate free from emotion and
fair in judgement
equitable reasonable and just
even-handed treating everyone
equally
impartial not favouring one more
than another

above board

290 faithful adj.

loyal

devoted very loyal or loving
dedicated devoting one's time and
energy to a special purpose
patriotic loyally supporting one's
country and its way of life
staunch dependably firm in attitude
steadfast firm; not changing or giving
way

291 fake adj.

sham

counterfeit made exactly like
something real in order to deceive
forged imitating for dishonest gain
fraudulent acting with intent to
deceive
imitating copying the appearance
spurious not what it claims to be

pseudo

292 false adj.

untrue

bogus pretended
ersatz used in imitation of the real
thing
fictitious untrue; invented
insincere not genuine in feeling,
manner or actions
mendacious telling lies; untruthful
trumped up invented or dishonest
excuse or accusation

assumed *phoney*

293 fame n.

renown

acclaim enthusiastic shout or
demonstration of welcome or
approval
celebrity state of being well known;
well-known person
eminence position of superiority;
distinction or high rank
notoriety state of being widely and
unfavourably known
prestige respect and influence
resulting from a good reputation
and/or past achievements
prominence importance; being
outstanding
reputation what is generally said or
believed about a person or thing
stardom position of being a top
performer

294 famous adj.

renowned   well-known

distinguished   outstanding for
  excellence
esteemed   thought very highly of
illustrious   very well known for great
  works

popular

295 fan n.

devotee   enthusiast   follower

admirer   person who regards another
  with pleasure, approval and respect
aficionado   keen and knowledgeable
  follower of a particular sport or
  pastime
champion   person who fights, argues
  or speaks in support of another, or of
  a cause
fanatic   person whose enthusiasm for
  something is beyond normal limits
partisan   strong and often uncritical
  supporter of a person, group, or cause
zealot   extremely enthusiastic and
  devoted supporter of a cause,
  especially a religious one

296 fantastic adj. (i)

illusory   *unreal*   *outlandish*
visionary   *whimsical*

297 fantastic adj. (ii)

excellent   *fabulous*   *wonderful*

298 far adj.

distant

far-flung   at or spread over a great
  distance
inaccessible   unable to be reached
remote   far away in place or time

back of beyond   *god-forsaken*

299 far-fetched adj.

improbable   *incredible*   *strained*
unlikely   *unnatural*

300 farm n.

croft   small enclosed field, next to a
  house, worked by the family
grange   country house with farm
  buildings that belong to it
hacienda   ranch or large estate in
  Spanish-speaking countries
homestead   farmhouse or similar
  building with the land and buildings
  round it
manor   large country house or the
  landed estate belonging to it
ranch   very large farm where sheep,
  cattle, horses, or other animals are
  bred
smallholding   piece of land of more
  than one acre in area, but usually less
  than 50 acres, sold or let for
  cultivation

301 fashion n. (i)

mode   style

craze   very popular fashion lasting
  only a short time
fad   short-lived but keenly followed
  interest or practice
trend-setter   person who leads the
  way in fashion
vogue   generally accepted fashion or
  custom at a certain time

fashion n. (ii)

manner   way

302 fast adj.

quick   rapid   speedy   swift

303 fasten v.

bond hold together, usually by glue
clamp hold things firmly by turning a screw
clasp grasp, hold, or embrace closely
clip fix or fasten with a small plastic or metal object
hitch fasten with a loop or hook
mitre join two pieces of wood or cloth so that their ends form a right angle
solder join metal parts together with a soft melted alloy
tack fasten with a small nail; sew temporarily with loose stitches
tether fasten an animal with a rope or chain to limit its movements

attach *cement* *glue*

304 fat adj.

obese

chubby having a round, usually pleasing, form
corpulent having a bulky body
flabby having too soft flesh
overweight weighing more than is normal or required
paunchy having a protruding belly
plump having a full, rounded shape
podgy short and fat
portly stout and dignified
stout solidly built and rather fat
tubby shaped like a tub

gross *pot-bellied*

305 fatal adj. (i)

deadly lethal mortal

toxic of, related to, or caused by poison
venomous poisonous; full of bitter feeling or hatred
virulent very powerful and dangerous; strongly and bitterly hostile

306 fatal adj. (ii)

disastrous

detrimental causing harm or damage
injurious hurtful; abusive or slanderous

calamitous *catastrophic* *ruinous*

307 fearful adj.

appalling shocking
dreadful very bad indeed; very shocking
frightful causing horror; ugly
terrible causing terror; very bad or incompetent
terrifying filling with very great fear

atrocious *ghastly* *hideous*

308 feather n.

crest tuft of feathers on a bird's head or on a helmet
down very fine, soft, furry feathers or short hairs
pinion end part of a bird's wing; the flight feathers
plumage general name for a bird's feathers
plume feather, especially a large or ornamental one
quill one of the large feathers on a bird's wing or tail

309 feed v.

board be supplied with daily meals in return for payment or services
browse feed as animals do, on leaves or grass
crop bite off and eat the crops of grass or plants grown as feed
foster promote the growth or development
graze eat growing grass
nourish keep alive and well by means of food
nurture care for, feed, and rear

310 feeling n.

consciousness state of mental awareness of oneself and one's surroundings
emotion instinctive feeling, such as love, hate, or grief
impression effect produced on the mind
inkling slight knowledge or suspicion; hint
intuition power of knowing or understanding something immediately without reasoning or being taught
passion intense emotion or obsession
premonition feeling that something is going to happen, usually unwelcome
sensation direct feeling, as of heat or pain, from the senses

foreboding *intimation* *presentiment*

311 few adj.

hardly any not many scarcely any some

meagre not enough in quantity, quality, or strength
scanty hardly enough
scarce not much or many compared with what is wanted
skimpy spending, providing, or using less than is really needed

312 fierce adj.

brutish very rough or very cruel
ferocious savagely fierce or cruel
murderous very dangerous, difficult, or unpleasant
savage uncontrollable and fiercely cruel
violent involving great force or strength
wild lacking restraint, discipline, or control

313 fight n.

affray fight in public between small groups
battle fight between large organized forces
bout boxing match
combat contest between two individuals, or two military forces
duel fight with guns or swords between two people

conflict *tussle*

314 find v.

chance upon *come across*
come upon *discover* *happen upon*
hit upon *light upon* *locate*

315 fine adj.

first-class *first-rate* *splendid*

316 finish v.

complete conclude end
get through terminate

achieve gain by effort
accomplish succeed in doing
seal settle solemnly

fulfil *round off*

317 fire n.

blaze bright flame or fire
combustion catching fire and burning
conflagration great and destructive fire
holocaust great destruction or loss of life, especially by fire

318 first adj.

best of the highest quality, value, or use

earliest   first to arrive
foremost   most important; leading; furthest forward
initial   of or belonging to the beginning
original   new in character or design
primary   earliest in time or order; first in a series
principal   chief; first in rank or importance

opening   *premier*

319   **fitting**   adj.

suitable

adapted   changed for a new use or situation
appropriate   right for its purpose
apt   exactly suitable for the circumstance or purpose
compatible   able to exist or be used together
pertinent   to the point
seemly   in accordance with the accepted standards of good taste

opportune

320   **flag**   n.

banner   strip of cloth with a sign, carried between two poles in a procession
Blue Peter   blue flag with a white square hoisted by a ship about to sail
colours   flag of a regiment or ship
ensign   flag flown by a ship to show what nation she belongs to
pennant   long, narrow, pointed flag
standard   distinctive flag used at ceremonies
tricolour   flag with three colours in stripes; French national flag

321   **flat**   adj.

level

horizontal   in a flat position, along or parallel to the ground
prone   lying flat
prostrate   stretched out face downwards
reclining   lying back
unbroken   not interrupted by humps or ridges

322   **flatter**   v.

compliment   express admiration; congratulate
fawn   try to win favour by overpraising or being insincerely attentive
praise   speak favourably and with admiration
toady to   be too nice to someone to gain personal advantage

pander to

323   **flow**   v.

cascade   pour or fall in quantity
flood   fill or become covered with water; overflow
glide   move noiselessly in a smooth, continuous and effortless manner
gush   flow or pour out suddenly
jet   shoot out forcefully from a small opening
ripple   form very small waves like wrinkles
rush   move suddenly with great speed
spout   come or pour out in a forceful stream
surge   move forward like powerful waves
trickle   flow or cause to flow in drops or a thin stream

324 flower n.

bloom

annual plant that lives for only one year or season
biennial plant that lives for two years, flowering and dying in the second
blossom mass of flowers appearing on a tree or bush
bouquet bunch of flowers for carrying in the hand
floret small flower, especially one making up the head of a composite flower, e.g., a daisy
nosegay small bunch of flowers, usually worn on a dress
perennial plant living for several years

325 flying adj.

drifting driven along as if by wind or waves
flapping waving slowly up and down or to and fro, making a noise
floating held up freely in air, gas, or liquid without sinking
fluttering moving the wings hurriedly in flying or trying to fly
gliding flying without engine power
hanging remaining in the air
hovering staying in the air in one place
planing flying without moving wings or using engines
skimming moving lightly and quickly near or just touching a surface
soaring rising high in flight
zooming moving quickly, especially with a buzzing sound

326 former adj.

previous

earlier   *late*   *one-time*   *past*

327 found v.

create cause something new to exist; produce something new
establish set up on a permanent basis
institute set up for the first time
originate begin or cause to begin
set up begin a new venture
start up set in motion; begin an activity

328 frank adj.

blunt rough and plain, without trying to be polite or kind
candid directly truthful, even when the truth is unwelcome
forthright direct and short in manner and speech
guileless lacking in cunning or deceit

artless   *outspoken*   *plain-spoken*
straight-forward   *uninhibited*

329 freely adv.

readily unreservedly

generously given readily and in large amounts
independently done on one's own without help from others
informally without ceremony
naturally without trying to look or sound different from usual
voluntarily willingly and without payment

330 friend n.

accomplice partner in wrongdoing
ally person who helps and supports another
chum close friend
companion person who escorts, attends or spends time with another
comrade friend and/or equal in work, play or war

crony   pal of long standing

collaborator   confederate

331 frown v.

glower   scowl sullenly
grimace   twist the face in pain or
   disgust, or to cause amusement

look black   *look daggers*

332 full adj.

filled

brimming   full to the top
chock-a-block   crammed or crowded
   together
gorged   choked up; stuffed full
satiated   cloyed with an excess of
   something

crammed   *glutted*   *jam-packed*

333 fun n.

*amusement   clowning   enjoyment
entertainment   fooling   gaiety
joking   jollity   merriment   mirth
play   playfulness   recreation
relaxation   teasing*

334 funny adj.

amusing   causing to laugh or smile
comical   amusing in an odd way
diverting   entertaining
hilarious   extremely funny
humorous   appealing to one's sense of
   fun
side-splitting   causing uncontrollable
   laughter

jocular   ludicrous

335 fuss n.

bother   pother

commotion   noisy confusion or
   excitement
flurry   state of troubled hurry and
   excitement
fluster   state of being hot, nervous,
   and confused

336 game n.

competition   friendly contest in which
   people try to do better than their
   rivals
contest   formal game between two or
   more people or teams
diversion   entertainment
match   game or sports event
regatta   races between rowing or
   sailing boats
sport   physical outdoor or indoor
   game with rules
tournament   contest of skill between
   players involving a series of matches

337 gasp v.

exclaim   utter suddenly because of
   strong feeling or pain
gulp   make a sudden swallowing
   movement of surprise or nervousness
heave   pant; strain one's throat as if
   vomiting
snort   make a rough noise by blowing
   air down the nose

338 gentle adj.

mild

compassionate   feeling pity and
   wishing to help others or show mercy
considerate   taking care not to
   inconvenience or hurt others
tender   easily moved to pity or
   sympathy
thoughtful   showing thought for the
   needs of others

soothing   tender-hearted

339 **get** v.
obtain

acquire gain possession of by one's
own efforts
appropriate take and use as one's
own without permission
benefit be given something useful,
profitable, or helpful
come by obtain something, especially
accidentally; find
fetch go for and bring back
gain get through one's own efforts
something desirable
inherit receive property, a title, or
possessions from someone who has
died
procure obtain by care or effort
receive accept or take in something
offered, sent, or given
secure become the possessor of,
especially as the result of effort
seize take possession of by force or
official order
take lay hold of; gain possession of
by force or effort

earn pocket purchase take home

340 **gift** n. (i)
present

bequest money, articles, or property
left to someone in a will
contribution something given or
supplied jointly with others
donation gift of money to a fund or
institution
dowry property or money brought
by a bride to her husband
endowment source of income
inheritance thing received from
someone who has died
offering contribution for a religious
purpose
voucher kind of ticket that can be
exchanged for certain goods or
services

alms dole gratuity tip

341 **gift** n. (ii)
talent

bent natural skill or liking
flair natural aptitude to do something
easily or select what is good
genius exceptional great inborn
ability

342 **girl** n.

adolescent young person between 13
and 16
child young female below the age of
puberty
juvenile young person
maid female servant doing indoor
work
maiden unmarried girl
minor person not yet reached the age
at which she is responsible in law for
her actions
tomboy girl who enjoys boyish
recreations

*lass lassie maidservant minx
miss wench*

343 **give** v.
bestow

allocate give as a share of something
available; set aside for a particular
purpose
assign set apart for a particular
function or event
award give by official decision as a
payment, penalty, or prize
contribute supply something jointly
with others
dispense deal out
donate make a gift to a fund or
institution
present give away, especially at a
ceremonial occasion

allot consign offer yield

344 glad adj.

well-pleased

delighted greatly pleased
elated filled with pride and joy
thrilled filled with emotion and
 excitement

gratified pleased as punch

345 gladly adv.

cheerfully *smilingly* *ungrudgingly*
willingly *with good grace*
with pleasure

346 glass n.

beaker tall drinking-cup, often
 without a handle
chalice vessel like a large goblet for
 holding wine
goblet drinking-glass with stem, foot
 and no handles
tumbler flat-bottomed drinking-glass
 with no handle or stem
wineglass glass, usually rounded,
 with a stem and base, for drinking
 wine from

347 go v.

advance move forward
decamp leave any place suddenly and
 secretly
depart go away from; leave
embark put or go on board ship at
 the start of a journey
make away go away in haste; steal or
 abduct

progress *set out* *travel*

348 good adj. (i)

virtuous

devout earnestly religious

honourable deserving respect
 because of good character
moral right and just
noble possessing excellent qualities,
 especially of character

high-minded *righteous* *saintly*

349 good adj. (ii)

beneficial causing a good result
desirable what is wanted
passable just good enough to be
 accepted
suitable good for its purpose

350 goods n.

chattels movable possessions
commodities useful things; articles of
 trade
merchandise goods for sale or trade
wares manufactured goods offered
 for sale

paraphernalia *produce* *stock*

351 grasp v. (i)

clasp clench grip seize

apprehend arrest and take into
 custody
clutch hold tightly
grapple seize and struggle with
hold take and keep in one's arms,
 hands, or teeth
nab seize as a thief
snatch take quickly or when a chance
 occurs

352 grasp v. (ii)

comprehend

apprehend grasp the meaning of;
 understand
realize understand and believe
 something

353 grass n.

green smooth stretch of grass for a special purpose

hay grass mown and dried for cattle food

herbage grass and other field plants

lawn area of closely-cut grass in a garden or park

meadow field of grass to make hay from

pasture land covered with grass and similar plants suitable for grazing cattle

turf soil with grass and roots growing in it

354 grassland n.

downs low rounded hills covered with grass, usually of chalk

heath area of flat, uncultivated land with low shrubs

moor wide, open, often raised area covered with heather, rough grass, and bushes

pampas large, grassy, treeless plains in South America

prairie large, treeless tract of land, especially in North America

savannah grassy plain in hot regions, with few or no trees

steppe large area of plain without trees in South-East Europe and Siberia

tundra vast, level, treeless Arctic regions where the subsoil is frozen

veld high, flat, open grassland in South Africa

wold area of open upland country

355 grave adj.

serious

grim stern in appearance

sedate dignified and not easily troubled

solemn not smiling or cheerful; dignified and impressive

sombre sadly serious

staid steady and unexciting in manner and taste

unsmiling

356 greedy adj. (i)

acquisitive keen to collect and own things

avaricious extremely greedy for riches

grasping avaricious; miserly

mercenary working only for money or other reward

rapacious taking everything one can, especially by force

venal easily bribed or corrupted

greedy adj. (ii)

gluttonous eating excessively

357 grey adj.

ashen *dove-grey* *gunmetal-grey*
leaden *pearly* *silvery* *smoky*

358 guard v.

keep safe   protect   watch over

conduct lead or guide

defend protect against attack

escort accompany as an honour, guide, protection, or to prevent escape

police control by, or as if, using police

shield protect or hide from harm, danger, or discovery

359 guess v.

conjecture

estimate calculate the value of something

reckon have as one's opinion

suppose   take as likely; consider as
 true or probable
surmise   give as a reasonable guess

speculate

360 **gun** n.

firearm

automatic   weapon that can be fired
 repeatedly by pressure on the
 trigger
blunderbuss   old type of gun with
 wide mouth, firing many balls at
 one shot
cannon   old type of large, heavy gun
 firing solid metal balls; automatic
 aircraft gun of large calibre
carbine   short, light automatic rifle of
 limited range
Colt   heavy revolver firing six bullets
howitzer   short, heavy gun firing
 shells high over a short distance
machine-gun   rapid-firing automatic
 gun, usually mounted, firing small
 ammunition
mortar   short, heavy gun for firing
 shells at a high angle
musket   early long-barrelled gun used
 before the invention of the rifle
pistol   small hand-gun
revolver   pistol with a revolving
 barrel
rifle   gun with long grooved barrel,
 fired from the shoulder
shotgun   gun for firing small shot at
 close range

361 **habit** n.

addiction   state of being utterly
 dependent on some habit,
 especially taking drugs
custom   usual way of behaving or
 doing something
dependence   condition of needing the
 help of and unable to do without
groove   a way of living that has
 become a habit; a rut

practice   habitual course of action
 that is accepted as correct
rut   habitual, usually dull, way of life
usage   customary manner of using or
 treating something

mania   *weakness for*

362 **hair** n.

curls   coiled locks of hair
down   very fine, soft short hairs
fleece   woolly hair of a sheep or
 similar animal
fur   soft, thick fine hair covering the
 bodies of certain animals
hide   animal skin, especially when
 used for leather
mane   long hair on a horse's or lion's
 neck
pelt   animal skin, especially with the
 fur or hair still on it
ringlets   long, hanging curls of hair
shock   bushy, untidy mass of hair
thatch   thick growth of hair on the
 head
tress   lock or plait of woman's hair

tonsure

363 **hang** v.

dangle   hang or swing loosely
droop   bend or hang downwards
string up   hang something high; kill
 by hanging
suspend   hang from above

364 **happen** v.

occur   take place

chance   take place by accident
come about   happen in due course of
 time
crop up   arise unexpectedly

befall   *transpire*

365 **happening** n.

event   incident   occurrence

accident something, especially something unpleasant or damaging, happening unexpectedly or by chance
circumstance one of the conditions or facts connected with an event or person
mishap unfortunate happening, usually not of a serious nature
phenomenon fact or event as it appears to the senses; remarkable person, thing or event

366 **hardly** adv.

barely   scarcely

367 **hastily** adv.

hurriedly

headlong falling or plunging forwards; in a hasty or rash way
precipitately rashly, hurriedly, and/or inconsiderately
promptly without delay

368 **hat** n.

beret round, soft flat cap with no peak
boater hard flat straw hat
bonnet hat with strings that tie under the chin
bowler hard felt hat with rounded top and brim, usually black
busby tall fur helmet worn by the Guards on ceremonial occasions
cap soft, flat head-covering without a brim but often with a peak
fez man's high, round flat-topped red cap with a tassel, worn by Muslims
head-dress ornamental covering or band worn on the head
mitre tall head-dress worn by bishops and abbots as a symbol of office
panama hat of fine pliant straw-like material
stetson hat with wide brim and high crown worn by cowboys
top hat man's tall, stiff silk, black or grey hat worn with formal dress
topper another word for top hat
toque woman's close-fitting brimless hat with a high crown
trilby man's soft felt hat with a lengthwise dent in the crown and a narrow brim

369 **hate** v.

loathe

abhor feel very great hatred
abominate have great hatred and dislike for
despise regard as inferior or worthless
detest dislike strongly
execrate curse; feel or express hatred

370 **have** v.

own possess, belong to
retain keep in one's possession or use; not lose

possess

371 **heap** n.

pile

accumulation an increasing quantity
hoard carefully saved and guarded store
load amount that can be carried
mass great quantity
stack orderly pile
supply stock or store; amount of something

batch   clump   cluster   collection

372 heartless adj.

cold-hearted hardened hard-hearted uncaring unfeeling unsympathetic

373 hearty adj.

affable showing warmth and friendliness
bouncy lively in manner and movement
buoyant light-hearted, cheerful, and hopeful
cordial good-tempered and friendly
whole-hearted with all one's ability, interest, and sincerity
zestful full of enthusiasm and enjoyment

374 help v.

aid assist

abet encourage or give help to a crime or criminal
accommodate oblige or do a favour for
collaborate work in partnership
contribute help to bring about
cooperate work or act together for a purpose
expedite make a plan or arrangement go faster
facilitate make easy or easier

befriend lend a hand succour

375 hide v.

conceal secrete

camouflage disguise or conceal objects by colouring or covering them, so that they blend into their surroundings
disguise change the appearance of
enshroud cover completely and hide

screen shelter, conceal, or protect
veil partly conceal

376 hill n.

bluff broad, steep headland, bank, or cliff
dune sand-hill piled up by wind on the seashore or in a desert
eminence piece of rising ground
foothill one of the low hills near the bottom of a mountain or range
hummock hump in the ground
knoll small, rounded hill
mound small hill; mass of piled-up earth or stones
tor prominent rock or heap of rocks, especially on a hill

377 hit v.

strike

batter hit hard and often
beat strike repeatedly, especially with a stick
belabour beat severely
bludgeon hit repeatedly with a heavy-headed stick
buffet hit, especially with the fist
clout give a hard blow with the hand
cuff strike lightly with the open hand
flay strip off the skin by whipping
flick strike or remove with a quick, light blow
flog beat severely with a whip or stick as a punishment
knock strike with a noisy, sharp blow
pummel hit repeatedly, especially with the fists
punch strike a quick, strong blow with the closed fist
scourge beat with a whip
slap strike quickly with the open hand

tap   knock gently; strike lightly
thrash   beat thoroughly; hit with
  repeated blows

club   rap   spank

378   holiday   n.

vacation

fête   outdoor entertainment, usually
  to raise funds
festival   religious or other celebration
field-day   day of much activity,
  especially of brilliant and exciting
  events
gala   joyous and festive organized
  occasion
jamboree   noisy, happy party

recess

379   home   n.

abode   dwelling place; house
accommodation   living premises
apartment   room or set of rooms for
  living in
bungalow   one-storeyed house
cottage   small, simple house usually
  in the country
domicile   dwelling-place; home
dwelling   place to live in
habitation   place to live in
housing estate   number of houses in
  an area planned as a unit
lodgings   room or rooms, not in a
  hotel, rented for living in
residence   place where one resides or
  lives, especially a grand one
rooms   set of rooms occupied by a
  person or family

*flat   caravan   house   maisonette
pad   penthouse   shack   shanty
tenement*

380   homely   adj.

plain

unaffected   natural in behaviour or
  character
unsophisticated   simple in ways and
  tastes

381   horse   n.

Arab   small, fast, intelligent breed of
  horse, originally from Arabia, used
  mainly for riding
bronco   wild or half-tamed horse of
  western North America
Clydesdale   heavy powerful breed of
  carthorse, originally from Scotland
cob   sturdy, short-legged horse for
  riding
mustang   small, wild horse of Mexico
  and south-west U.S.A.
nag   horse spoken of in a slighting
  way
piebald   horse with irregular patches
  of white and black or other dark
  colour
shire   large powerful English
  carthorse
skewbald   horse marked or spotted in
  white and any colour except black
thoroughbred   bred of pure or
  pedigree stock

382   however   adv.

*all the same   even so
in whatever way   nevertheless
to whatever extent*

383   hurt   v.

injure   damage
ache   suffer a continuous dull pain
burn   injure by fire or acid; be
  unpleasantly hot

smart   feel a stinging pain, not lasting
  long
sting   feel or cause to feel sharp pain
  in one particular place
throb   giving pain in a strong, quick,
  steady rhythm
wound   injure by a cut, stab, blow or
  tear

bruise

384   idea   n.

conception   act of forming an idea or
  plan
impression   uncertain idea, belief, or
  remembrance
notion   vague idea or opinion, often
  incorrect
theory   reasonable explanation of
  something for which certain proof is
  still needed
viewpoint   way of considering or
  judging a thing or person

385   if   conj.

even though   *granting*
in the event that   *on condition*
providing   *supposing*   *whether*

386   ignore   v.

disregard   take no notice of

brush aside   reject casually or curtly
cold-shoulder   treat with deliberate
  unfriendliness
neglect   give no or too little attention
  or care to
omit   leave not done or fail to do
slight   treat rudely, without respect,
  or as if unimportant
snub   reject or humiliate a person by
  treating him scornfully
turn a blind eye   know what is
  happening, but choose to ignore it

387   ill   adj.

poorly   sick   sickly   unwell

ailing   unwell, especially over a long
  period
diseased   affected with an unhealthy
  condition
indisposed   slightly ill
infirm   weak in body or mind,
  especially from age or illness
unhealthy   not having or not showing
  good health

bedridden   *laid up*

388   imaginary   adj.

fanciful   using the imagination freely
illusory   deceiving and unreal

389   improve   v. (i)

make better

rectify   put right
redress   put right a wrong or an
  injustice
reform   make or become better by
  removing faults
regenerate   make better morally; give
  new life or vigour to

reconstruct   *remodel*   *reorganize*

improve   v. (ii)

get better

recover

390   in   prep.

during   *in the midst of*
in the thick of   *on the inside of*
within

391   inaudible   adj.

faint   not clearly heard

imperceptible   too slight to be heard
indistinct   not able to be heard clearly
muted   deadened or muffled
unclear   not able to be understood

392   incidentally   adv.

by the way

casually   in passing

393   increase   v.

enlarge   make greater

amass   gather in great amounts
amplify   make fuller, larger, or
  greater; add details to
augment   increase in size, amount, or
  quality
expand   make or grow larger
extend   make longer in space or time;
  increase the scope of
supplement   make additions to

394   incurable   adj.

fatal   causing or ending in death
inoperable   unable to be cured by
  surgery
terminal   related to an illness that will
  cause death

395   indeed   adv.

*admittedly   assuredly   in fact
in truth   really   truly*

396   indirect   adj.

circuitous   roundabout
divergent   going in different
  directions from a point
erratic   irregular or uneven
meandering   wandering in a leisurely,
  aimless way
out-of-the-way   distant; uncommon

tortuous   full of twists and turns; not
  straightforward

wandering   zigzag

397   individual   adj.

characteristic   typical or distinctive
distinct   definite and unmistakable
inherent   forming a natural part of
personal   belonging to oneself

398   indulgent   adj.

complacent   self-satisfied
forgiving   ceasing to feel angry or
  bitter towards
lax   careless or lazy; not strict or
  severe
lenient   merciful, especially when
  awarding punishment
permissive   allowing a great deal of,
  or too much, freedom
tolerant   able to put up with the
  beliefs, actions, or opinions of
  others without protest

self-gratifying   spoilt

399   infamous   adj.

of ill repute

notorious   widely and unfavourably
  known
reprehensible   deserving to be blamed
  or scolded
scandalous   shocking to feelings of
  what is right or proper

abhorrent

400   infect   v.

blight   spoil plants through disease
  causing withering
contaminate   make impure by mixing
  with dirty or poisonous matter
corrupt   turn from good to bad
degrade   change from a higher to a

lower kind of living matter; change
for the worse
pollute make dirty or impure,
especially by adding harmful or
offensive substances
taint affect with a trace of some bad
quality, decay, or infection

401 insist v.

assert state forcibly
claim demand as the rightful owner
or one's right; state as a fact
declare state with great force; make
known publicly or officially
emphasize give special importance to
certain words or details
maintain assert as true

402 inspire v.

animate bring or give life
exhilarate make very happy or lively
impress make a person form a strong,
usually favourable, opinion of
something
invigorate give new strength and
courage to

hearten *uplift*

403 instant adj.

instantaneous occurring or done at
once

expeditious *immediate* *prompt*

404 instead adv.

as an alternative to
as a substitute for *in place of*
in preference to *preferably*
rather than

405 intact adj.

complete *sound* *unchanged*
undamaged *untouched* *whole*

406 intend v.

contemplate think about, have in
view as a possibility
propose declare as one's plan; suggest
resolve decide firmly
scheme plan in a secret or underhand
way

aim at *aspire to* *have in mind* *plan*

407 interesting adj.

absorbing taking all one's attention
engrossing occupying one's attention
completely
fascinating having great attraction
intriguing rousing curiosity
riveting holding firmly, usually in
fascinated attention or horror

diverting *entertaining* *spell-binding*
thought-provoking

408 invent v.

devise

compose make up or form; write
music, poetry, or stories
create bring into existence; produce
design draw or plan out for a specific
purpose
discover find out or find, especially
for the first time

conjure up

409 island n.

isle

archipelago group of many small
islands
atoll ring-shaped coral reef enclosing
a lagoon
islet small island
reef line of rocks, coral, or sand at,
or near, the surface of the sea

410 jab v.

dig poke, especially in the ribs
elbow push with one's elbows
prod push with a finger or pointed
  object
thrust push forcibly and suddenly as
  with a sword or knife

411 jagged adj.

notched having V-shaped cuts or
  indentations
ragged torn or frayed
ridged formed into narrow, raised
  strips
serrated having a series of small
  projections like the teeth of a saw
uneven not level or smooth; varying

craggy saw-toothed

412 jail n.

gaol prison

detention centre place where young
  offenders may be kept for short
  periods
lock-up room or small building
  where prisoners can be kept for a
  short time
penal institution place of punishment
  awarded by law
penitentiary State or federal prison in
  America
police station office of a local police
  force

413 jaunty adj.

bouncy self-confident

buoyant light-hearted and cheerful
sprightly gay and light in manner and
  movement

eager jolly

414 jealous adj.

covetous desiring eagerly, especially
  something belonging to another
  person
envious feeling discontented about
  someone else's qualities or possessions
possessive unwilling to share one's
  things with other people

green-eyed suspicious

415 job n.

work

chore small, routine and tedious
  task, especially a domestic one
employment work done to earn a
  living
livelihood way one earns enough to
  pay for what is necessary
occupation activity that keeps a
  person busy; one's employment
office position of authority or trust
trade business, especially buying,
  selling, or exchanging products or
  goods
vocation urge to follow a particular
  career, especially one to serve others

appointment

416 join v.

connect join, link or fasten together
fasten make or become firmly fixed
  or closed
link make or be a connection
  between
splice join by overlapping or weaving
  ends together
unite make or become one

bolt together chain rivet weld

417 joke n.

jest

chestnut stale old joke or story

gag   joke or funny story, especially as part of a comedian's act
quip   witty or sarcastic remark
wisecrack   quick, short, clever remark
witticism   sharp, funny, intelligent remark

spoof   whimsy

418   journey   n.

excursion   short journey for pleasure
expedition   journey or voyage for a particular purpose
globe-trotting   travelling all over the world, especially as a tourist
jaunt   short trip, especially one taken for pleasure
outing   short outward and return journey for pleasure
pilgrimage   journey made to a place as a mark of respect
quest   journey in search of something
safari   trip to hunt or explore, especially in East Africa
tour   journey through a country, town or building; visiting various places or things of interest
trek   long and often difficult journey
trip   any tour or journey, especially for pleasure
voyage   journey, especially a long one by sea or air

cruise

419   jump   v.

leapfrog   jump astride over someone's back; overtake one after the other
pounce   spring or swoop down on and grasp
vault   jump over, using the hands or a pole to gain more height

bounce   bound   hop   leap   spring

420   junk   n.

cast-offs   dregs   garbage   leavings
left-overs   odds and ends   refuse
rejects   remnants   rubbish   scraps
second-hand goods   trash   waste

421   just   adj.

fair

disinterested   acting fairly because not influenced by personal advantage
impartial   unprejudiced; unbiased
neutral   without any feelings on either side of a question
objective   not influenced by personal feelings
open-minded   receptive to new ideas
unprejudiced   fair in judgement
upright   strictly honourable

422   keep   v.

fulfil   carry out
maintain   keep in good condition
manage   have under effective control
preserve   keep safe; keep in an unchanged condition
store   put away for future use

hold on to   stock

423   kill   v.

assassinate   kill an important person by violent means
execute   put a condemned person to death
hang   kill by suspending from a rope that tightens round the neck
liquidate   get rid of, especially by killing
murder   kill a person unlawfully and on purpose
remove   do away with

silence force to stop expressing opinions or making opposing statements, usually by killing

bump off *knock off* *polish off* *slay* *snuff out*

424 **kind** n.

sort type

genre particular style of art or literature
genus group of animals or plants with common characteristics, usually containing several species
order group of plants or animals classified as similar in many ways
species group of plants or animals alike in all important ways, and able to breed together
variety type which is different from others in the group to which it belongs

breed *clan* *kin* *stock* *tribe*

425 **king** n.

crowned head   monarch   sovereign

potentate ruler with direct power over his people
supreme head highest in authority or rank

majesty *ruler*

426 **knife** n.

bayonet long knife fixed to the end of a rifle
bowie knife strong hunting knife with short hilt and a guard for the hand
cutlass short, heavy sword with a slightly curved blade
jack-knife large folding pocket knife
machete broad heavy-bladed knife used in Central America as a tool and weapon

rapier long, light, thin double-edged sword with sharp point
sabre cavalry sword with a curved blade
scimitar short, curved oriental sword
stiletto small dagger with a slender, tapered blade
switchblade weapon with a blade that springs out when a button is pressed; flick-knife
tomahawk fighting axe of North American Indians

dagger *dirk*

427 **know** v. (i)

comprehend grasp mentally
fathom get at the true meaning of
grasp succeed in understanding
understand perceive the meaning of

appreciate *be aware of*
be conscious of *be familiar with*
feel certain *have in one's head*

know v. (ii)

recognize know again; identify from one's previous knowledge or experience

428 **knowledge** n.

education systematic instruction designed to give knowledge and develop skill
erudition great learning
data facts as information
instruction process of teaching; advice on how to do something
learning deep knowledge gained by study
scholarship great learning in a particular academic subject
schooling being taught in a school; training of an animal

429 land n.

cape high land jutting out into the sea
continent one of the seven main land masses of the earth
country nation or state; the land it occupies
ground earth or soil; surface of the earth
homeland country of one's birth or where one lives
isthmus narrow area of land with sea on each side joining two land masses
mainland country or continent without its adjacent islands
peninsula piece of land projecting far into the sea that is almost surrounded by water
terrain stretch of land, with regard to its natural features

mother country   native land
terra firma

430 lasting adj.

enduring

immortal living or continuing for ever; famous for all time
imperishable which will not wear out or decay
indestructible incapable of being broken up; very long-lasting
persisting continuing, especially past expected time

long-lived   never-ending   unending

431 lastly adv.

finally in conclusion

hindmost   in last place   rearmost

432 late adj.

behind time

overdue left unpaid too long; later than expected

tardy slow or late to act, move, or happen
unpunctual not arriving or doing things at the appointed time

behind schedule

433 lately adv.

a little while back   a short time ago
not long before   of late
recently

434 laugh v.

chuckle laugh softly or to oneself
giggle laugh in a silly or nervous way
guffaw laugh crudely and noisily
roar laugh long and loudly
shriek laugh shrilly
snigger giggle in a disrespectful, sly way
titter snigger in a disrespectful, very quiet way

cackle   chortle   split one's sides

435 lazy adj.

idle   indolent   slothful

lethargic extremely lacking in energy
shiftless lacking in purpose, ability, or effort
slack not properly careful or quick
sluggish slow-moving; not alert or active
unambitious without desire for success, power, or riches
unenterprising lacking in initiative and readiness to undertake or experiment
unindustrious lacking the will to work hard

easy-going

436 lest conj.

for fear that   in case
so as to avoid the risk of

437 let v. (i)

allow   permit

assent to   agree to
authorize   give power to or
  permission for
empower   give someone the power or
  lawful right
sanction   accept, approve, or permit

allow to pass

438 let v. (ii)

lease   rent

charter   let or hire a ship, aircraft, or
  vehicle
contract   arrange or undertake by
  formal agreement
hire out   allow the temporary use for
  payment
lend   allow someone the use of
  something for a time without
  payment
sublet   let accommodation that one is
  renting oneself

439 liar n.

fibber   prevaricator

false witness   person who gives false
  evidence in a law court
libeller   person who publishes a false
  statement about another
perjurer   person who deliberately
  gives false evidence while on oath

story-teller

440 lie v. (i)

laze   spend time in idle relaxation
loll   stand, sit, lean, or rest in a lazy,
  loose position

recline   lean backwards; lie down
repose   lie still and comfortably at rest
sprawl   stretch oneself out slackly and
  awkwardly

relax

lie v. (ii)

fib   prevaricate; speak untruthfully

441 lift v.

elevate   raise

brandish   wave a thing in display or
  threateningly
hoist   raise or haul up; lift with ropes
  and pulleys
lever   move or force open by a bar
  pivoted on a fixed point
uphold   support; keep from falling

raise aloft   *raise high*

442 like v.

be fond of

delight in   take great pleasure in
enjoy   get happiness from
fancy   wish for; have a liking for
feel inclined   have a willingness to
relish   enjoy greatly

take pleasure in

443 likely adj.

probable

conceivable   able to be imagined or
  believed
imaginable   able to be pictured in the
  mind
promising   likely to turn out well or
  produce good results

444 likeness n.

resemblance   similarity

copy   thing made to look like another
facsimile   reproduction of a
  document, book or painting
reproduction   copy of a painting, or
  piece of furniture, made in imitation
  of an earlier style

445 liking n.

favouritism   unfairly generous
  treatment
fondness   having a gentle and tender
  liking for
penchant   strong leaning towards
preference   desire for one thing rather
  than another
taste   personal liking

attachment   attraction   regard

446 list n.

catalogue   list of items, usually in a
  special order and with a description
  of each
directory   book containing names,
  addresses, and telephone numbers of
  individuals or firms
index   alphabetical list at the back of a
  book of the main names and subjects
  in it, and the pages where they can
  be found
inventory   detailed list of goods or
  furniture
line-up   row of people or things got
  together for a particular purpose
register   official list of names, items,
  or attendances
roll   official list or register, especially
  with names
roster   list showing people's turns of
  duty

447 little adj.

small

diminutive   remarkably small
petite   small, dainty build applied to a
  woman
stunted   not properly or fully-grown
tiny   very small

*bantam   dwarfish   light-weight
midget   pigmy*

448 liveable adj.

bearable   able to be put up with
habitable   suitable for living in;
  inhabitable
occupiable   able to be lived in for the
  time but without comfort

449 lively adj.

full of life

animated   full of spirit and excitement
brisk   quick and active in movement
frisky   playful

enthusiastic

450 load n.

*boatload   burden   cargo   contents
freight   lorryload   merchandise
shipload   waggonload*

451 lonely adj. (i)

estranged   cold and unfriendly
outcast   driven out or rejected
solitary   alone, without companions;
  fond of being alone

*alone   companionless   friendless
unwanted*

452 lonely adj. (ii)

*deserted   remote   unfrequented
uninhabited*

453 look v.

behold see; observe
glance give a quick, brief look
glimpse catch a brief view of
glower stare hard and sullenly
leer give a sideways, sneering, or
 suggestive look or grin
peep look through a narrow opening,
 or from a concealed place
peer look searchingly or with
 difficulty
regard look upon in a particular way
scowl make an angry or threatening
 frown

454 look for v (i)

cast around for hunt for
search for seek

455 look for v. (ii)

anticipate regard as likely; foresee
expect believe that something will
 happen
reckon on count or depend on

456 loose adj.

*detached slack unattached
unchained unclasped unconnected
unfastened unfettered unhooked
unrestrained untied*

457 lot n.

*considerable number good deal
heap large quantity load mass
pile stack tons*

458 love v.

adore love deeply; worship as divine
adulate flatter or praise excessively
be infatuated with be filled
 temporarily with an intense,
 unreasoning love for a person or
 thing

care for feel affection for
cherish look after lovingly
crave for long for intensely
desire want very much
have a crush on have a strong,
 foolish and short-lived liking or
 love for someone
hold dear regard highly and with
 reverence
idolize feel excessive admiration or
 devotion
lust for strong or excessive desire,
 especially sexual
pine for feel great longing for
 something, usually unattainable
worship honour or adore as a god
yearn for have a strong, loving, and
 sad desire for

think the world of treasure

459 lovely adj.

attractive pleasing in appearance or
 effect
beautiful giving great pleasure to the
 senses
becoming looking very well on the
 wearer
charming arousing liking or
 admiration
comely good-looking
delightful giving great pleasure
glamorous romantically fascinating
pretty pleasing or appealing in a
 delicate or graceful way

*alluring enchanting fascinating
good-looking ravishing seductive
sexy*

460 luckily adv.

by good fortune fortunately
happily

461 **lure** v.

attract get the attention of
decoy deceive a person or animal
 into danger
entice attract or persuade by offering
 something pleasant
inveigle trick someone into doing
 something
tempt arouse a desire

ensnare

462 **mad** adj.

angry irate

enraged very angry
frantic wildly excited or agitated by
 anxiety
fuming seething with anger
furious violently angry
indignant angry because of
 something unjust or wicked
infuriated intensely angry
irritated impatient or slightly angry
 at small things
nettled stung by unkind or
 thoughtless remarks or actions
raging violently and noisily angry
riled stirred up and agitated
vexed worried and annoyed

cross peeved peevish raving

463 **magnificent** adj.

awe-inspiring filling with respect,
 fear and wonder
glorious having, or worthy of, great
 fame, honour, or beauty
luxurious very fine, costly, and
 extremely comfortable
majestic stately and dignified;
 imposing
noble possessing excellent qualities,
 especially in one's character; free
 from pettiness, or meanness
regal like or fit for a king

sublime of the very highest or most
 impressive kind
sumptuous expensive or extravagant

*gorgeous grand great splendid
superb*

464 **main** adj.

chief principal

crucial of deciding importance
paramount supreme
predominant greater than others in
 power, influence, number or intensity
primary of the first importance

465 **mainly** adv.

chiefly mostly principally

*by and large especially
for the most part on the whole
primarily*

466 **make** v.

assemble gather or put together
build make by putting parts or
 materials together
construct make by putting together
 or combining parts
devise think out, plan, or invent
draw up prepare a draft, usually of a
 legal document
erect set up or build
manufacture produce on a large scale
 by machinery
produce make or bring into existence
 from materials, labour, or thought

467 **manner** n.

custom usual way of behaving or
 doing something
method way of doing something
mode way in which a thing is done;
 current fashion

technique   method in which a skilled activity is carried out
style   manner of writing, speaking, or doing something
system   ordered set of ideas, methods, or ways of working

468   **many**   adj.

numerous

innumerable   too many to be counted
multitudinous   very large in number
sundry   a few; varying
various   more than one; individual and separate

469   **map**   n.

atlas   book of maps
chart   map designed for navigators on water or in the air
gazeteer   book or section of book that lists and describes places
graph   diagram showing the relationship between two sets of quantities
grid   network of squares on maps, numbered for reference
plan   map of a town or district
projection   representation of the surface of the earth on a plane surface
relief map   map showing hills and valleys either by shading or moulding
topographical map   map showing details of the surface features of a region

470   **marvellous**   adj.

astounding   breathtaking   extraordinary   miraculous   remarkable   unheard-of   unparalleled   unprecedented

471   **mature**   adj.

fully developed   full-grown

adult   full-grown person or animal
full-blown   developed to its fullest and best extent
ripe   ready to be gathered and used
seasoned   brought into a fit condition for use by drying, treating, or allowing to ripen

ready

472   **maybe**   adv.

perhaps

as the case may be   for all I know possibly

473   **mean**   adj. (i)

catchpenny   worthless, but appearing attractive through cheapness or showiness
cheap   low in price; good value
inferior   not good or less good in quality or value
low-grade   low in quality or standard
meretricious   attractive on the surface, but of no value or importance
shabby   appearing poor because of wear
shoddy   made or done cheaply and badly
tatty   untidy and uncared for
tawdry   cheaply showy, but without real value
worthless   not worth anything; useless

474   **mean**   adj. (ii)

ungenerous

grudging   resenting having to give or allow something
miserly   hoarding money and spending as little as possible
narrow-minded   considering only

part of a question or favouring only one opinion

petty having a limited, ungenerous mind
small-minded narrow or selfish in outlook

mean-spirited

475 meek adj.

humble

forbearing patient and long-suffering
lowly simple and plain in manner
unprotesting accepting things without complaint

476 meet v.

accost go up and speak to, especially boldly
chance upon come upon by chance
encounter meet unexpectedly
face meet or oppose firmly and not try to avoid
respond to speak or act in answer to

face up to *make the acquaintance of*
run across

477 meeting n.

assembly people meeting for a special purpose
conference meeting for discussion and exchange of opinions
congregation group of people worshipping together
congress formal meeting of a group of people with a shared purpose
convention large formal meeting of a group with common interests
reception formal party held to receive guests
rendezvous arrangement to meet, or the place chosen to meet
tryst appointment to meet secretly

gathering *get-together*

478 mend v.

repair

remedy put or make right
restore bring back to its original state by repairing or rebuilding

fix up *patch up* *put back together*
put right

479 merely adj. & adv.

just *nothing more than* *only*
simply *solely*

480 messy adj.

untidy

chaotic in a state of complete disorder and confusion
dishevelled ruffled and untidy in appearance
filthy disgustingly dirty
frowsy shabby and untidy
slovenly unclean and untidy in appearance
unkempt looking neglected

frumpy *sloppy*

481 mind n.

common sense practical good sense and judgement
consciousness awareness of one's self and surroundings
intellect mind's power to reason and acquire knowledge
intelligence ability to reason
mentality one's characteristic attitude of mind; outlook
sanity soundness of mind; freedom from lasting mental disturbance

brain-power

482 miser n.

scrooge *skinflint*

483 **miserly** adj.

niggardly unwilling to spend money
parsimonious extremely careful or
reluctant in spending
stingy grudging in spending and
giving
tight-fisted mean with money and
possessions

*cheese-paring frugal money-
grubbing penny-pinching*

484 **mist** n.

fog thick mist that is difficult to see
through
haze light mist or smoke
smog fog polluted by smoke and
chemical fumes
vapour particles of moisture or other
substance suspended in air and visible
as clouds or smoke

485 **mistake** n.

error

blunder mistake made especially
through ignorance or carelessness
boob stupid embarrassing mistake
fallacy false idea or belief
faux pas embarrassing social mistake
or indiscretion
gaffe tactless remark
inaccuracy error or slip in fact or
calculation
miscalculation incorrect estimate
misunderstanding failure to
understand correctly
oversight unintended failure to notice
or do something

486 **modern** adj.

up-to-date

avant-garde producing or using an
ultra-modern style, especially in art
or literature

contemporary belonging to the same
period, present or past
novel new, especially clever or
unfamiliar
topical related to, dealing with, or
being a subject of present interest

*experimental present-day
the latest thing*

487 **modest** adj.

unassuming

humble having or showing a low
opinion of one's own importance
self-effacing avoiding the attention of
others
unpretentious not showy or
pompous

488 **mountain** n.

alp mountain peak; pasture-land on
mountains in Switzerland
butte isolated, steep-sided, flat-
topped hill
chain number of connected
mountains
escarpment long, continuous steep
face of a ridge or plateau
highlands mountainous country
peak pointed top, especially of a
mountain
precipice very steep or vertical face
of a cliff or rock
range connected line of mountains or
hills
sierra low range or area of sharply-
pointed mountains in Spain or
Spanish America
summit top, especially the highest
part on the top of a mountain

489 **much** adj.

a great deal

abundant more than enough

ample quite enough
bountiful given generously
considerable fairly large in amount
or size
plentiful in large quantities or
numbers

490 **muddled** adj.
confused   disordered

botched spoilt by poor or clumsy
work
bungled tackled clumsily and
without success
disarranged out of order or position
disorderly lacking order and tidiness
disorganized lacking orderly system
jumbled mixed in a confused way
snarled jammed and difficult to free
tangled twisted into a confused mass

491 **muddy** adj.

miry deeply and stickily muddy
mucky very dirty and messy
sludgy greasy and muddy
slushy covered in partly-melted and
often muddy snow

boggy   *marshy*   *swampy*

492 **must** v.

be compelled to be forced to
be obliged to have a duty to; bound
to do
have to be obliged to
ought to have a duty to; be advised
to

493 **nag** v.

badger annoy with frequent requests
or questions
carp keep finding unnecessary fault

grumble complain in a bad-tempered
way
hector torment by teasing

bully

494 **naked** adj.
nude

stark-naked completely without
clothes

in one's birthday suit   *in the altogether*
in the raw   *unclothed*   *undressed*
without a stitch on

495 **name** v.

address speak to; refer to in
speaking; deliver a speech to
appoint put in or choose for a
position, job, or purpose
baptize give a name to at a Christian
ceremony
call name; describe or address as
christen give a Christian name to in
baptism; give a nickname to
entitle give a name to a book, poem,
or picture
identify recognize as being a
particular person or thing
mention speak or write about briefly;
refer to by name
nominate suggest or appoint
someone to a position
specify refer to exactly

496 **nameless** adj.
anonymous

obscure not at all well-known;
unimportant
undesignated without a special name
or description
unidentified not recognized as being
a certain person or thing
unknown not known to anyone
unspecified referred to but not
described

497 namely adv.

as a case in point   for instance
specifically   that is   that is to say

498 nasty adj. (i)

disgusting very unpleasant; against
  one's principles
indecent offending against what is
  fitting and proper
objectionable causing disapproval
obnoxious extremely unpleasant
unsavoury morally unpleasant or
  unacceptable

blasphemous   foul-mouthed
revolting   sickening

499 nasty adj. (ii)
unkind   unpleasant

despicable deserving to be despised
ill-natured bad-tempered and unkind
malicious wishing or intending to
  hurt others
spiteful desiring to annoy or hurt in
  small ways
surly bad-tempered and unfriendly
vicious wicked or violently cruel

500 nature n.

character qualities that make a
  person or thing different from others
disposition person's usual frame of
  mind; temperament
personality distinctive qualities of a
  person
temperament person's nature as it
  controls the way he behaves, feels and
  thinks

make-up

501 naughty adj. (i)

defiant fearlessly refusing to obey
delinquent breaking the law or doing
  socially unacceptable things
disobedient failing or refusing to
  obey
exasperating annoying greatly
impish annoying in a harmless way
mischievous teasing or annoying
  playfully
reprehensible deserving to be told off
  or blamed
roguish playfully naughty in a
  deliberate and affected way

undisciplined   unruly   wayward

502 naughty adj. (ii)
improper

risqué slightly indecent
smutty morally improper
titillating pleasantly exciting or
  stimulating

503 nearly adv.
almost

all but   just about   more or less
not quite   roughly

504 neglect v.

abstain from keep oneself from doing
disregard pay no attention to; treat
  as of no importance
ignore take no notice of; pretend not
  to know or see
overlook fail to observe or consider
shun keep away from
spurn reject scornfully

505 nevertheless adv. & conj.
however   in any case   in spite of
none the less   not withstanding

506 newspaper n.

daily newspaper sold every day except Sunday and perhaps Saturday
tabloid newspaper with a small page size
weekly newspaper or magazine appearing once a week

507 next adj. (i)

adjacent adjoining bordering

next adj. (ii)

after ensuing following subsequent

508 nice adj.

agreeable pleasant pleasing

amusing causing smiles or laughter
attractive pleasing in appearance or effect
delightful highly pleasing
enjoyable giving pleasure
friendly kindly and helpful

*amiable charitable cheering
congenial generous kindly
likeable satisfactory sympathetic
understanding warm-hearted*

509 noise n.

bedlam wild, noisy place or activity; madhouse
clamour loud, continuous, confused noise, especially of shouting
clang loud, ringing sound
din loud echoing and annoying noise
hubbub loud, confused noise of voices
hullabaloo loud, confused noise of voices protesting
pandemonium wild and noisy confusion

racket noisy disturbance
uproar outburst of noise from excitement or anger

jangle jingle rattle

510 none pron.

no-one no part not a bit not any not one

511 nonsense n.

absurdity funny or foolish thing because clearly unsuitable
claptrap worthless talk or ideas used only to win applause
drivel silly and meaningless talk
gibberish meaningless sounds
gobbledegook pompous language used by officials
ridiculousness talk or actions deserving to be laughed at
stupidity sayings or actions lacking in common sense

*balderdash craziness
stuff and nonsense tommyrot*

512 note v.

record write down

annotate add short notes of explanation
catalogue make a list of places, names, or goods in a special order
chronicle record historical events in the order they happened
enter put details in a list or book
insert put extra detail between lines already written
register put into an official record

513 notorious adj.

of ill repute

disreputable having a bad reputation

infamous   being widely known for wicked behaviour
stigmatized   branded as something shameful

514   **now**   adv.

*at present   immediately
straight away*

515   **object**   v.

demur   show signs of being against something
disapprove   have or express an unfavourable opinion
dissent   have or express a different opinion
expostulate   make a friendly protest; reason or argue with a person
oppose   argue or fight against
protest   express annoyance or disagreement
remonstrate   argue in protest

516   **obsolete**   adj.

antiquated   old and not suited to present needs or conditions
discontinued   no longer made or offered for sale
outdated   no longer in general use
outmoded   no longer in fashion
redundant   surplus to requirements; no longer needed for any available job

517   **obvious**   adj.
evident   manifest

explicit   clear and fully expressed
palpable   easily perceived by the senses; easily understood
patent   easy to see; unconcealed
recognizable   knowable from one's previous knowledge or experience

*clear as crystal   clear-cut
plain as a pikestaff*

518   **odd**   adj.
strange   unusual

abnormal   different from what is ordinary or expected
eccentric   different from the usual in behaviour and dress; odd
grotesque   very odd or unnatural
incongruous   comparing strangely with what surrounds it
queer   differing from the normal in a strange way
unconventional   not following the accepted customs, especially in an original way
unorthodox   not generally or officially accepted

*bizarre   capricious   idiosyncratic
peculiar*

519   **offend**   v.

affront   be rude to or hurt the feelings of, especially in public
disgust   cause a very strong feeling of dislike and/or indignation
humiliate   cause to feel disgraced
insult   treat with scorn and abuse
provoke   make angry; rouse to action
repulse   refuse coldly

520   **official**   adj.

authorized   granted official permission
authoritative   recognized as being true or reliable
certified   declared formally as being correct
lawful   permitted by law
legitimate   in accordance with the law, or with certain rules or standards
sanctioned   formally accepted or approved

*accredited   approved   governmental
legal   licensed*

521 officious adj.

inquisitive excessively curious,
  especially about the affairs of others;
  eager to learn
interfering pushing oneself into
  someone else's affairs
meddlesome often interfering in
  people's affairs
prying finding out secretly about
  someone else's private affairs

bossy nosey

522 often adv.

frequently

generally as a rule; commonly
habitually regularly out of habit
periodically at regular intervals
usually normally; on most occasions

repeatedly

523 once adv. & conj.

on one occasion

formerly in earlier times
previously coming before in time or
  order

524 opinion n.

assessment estimate of the worth,
  quality or likelihood of
assumption something taken as a fact
  without proof
attitude manner of thinking, feeling,
  or behaving
belief feeling that something is true or
  real
conviction firm opinion or belief
feeling idea or belief not wholly
  based on reason
impression effect produced on the
  mind; uncertain idea, belief or
  remembrance
judgement ability to use good sense

to achieve a balanced view point
observation comment or remark
stance way of thinking; mental
  attitude
standpoint position from which
  things are seen and opinions formed
view personal opinion about
  something

525 order n. (i)

command

dictate order which should be obeyed
directive general instruction issued
  by authority
instructions statements making
  known to a person what he is required
  to do; directions
regulation official rule
request something asked for,
  especially politely

526 order n. (ii)

sequence

grouping planned arrangement of
  things within units
harmony agreement in action,
  opinion, or feeling
symmetry similarity or balance
  between the parts of something
tidiness neat and orderly
  arrangement
uniformity state in which everything
  is unvarying

orderliness

527 ordinary adj.

common normal

commonplace well-known and
  lacking originality
conventional following accepted
  practices and customs too closely
familiar well-known; usual

prevailing   most common or general
typical   combining and showing the
main signs of a particular kind,
group, or class

*common-or-garden   everyday
run-of-the-mill*

528   pain   n.

ache   dull, continuous pain
agony   extreme mental or physical
suffering
anguish   extreme misery or grief
colic   severe pain in the stomach and
bowels
discomfort   not being easy in body or
mind
pang   sudden, sharp feeling of pain in
body or mind
soreness   tenderness of a wound,
injury, or muscle
stitch   sudden, sharp pain in the
muscles at the side of the body
suffering   general pain, misery, or
grief
twinge   sudden, brief, darting, or
stabbing pain

heartache

529   pale   adj.

anaemic   pale and sickly-looking;
lacking vigour and vitality
ashen   drained of colour; pale grey
colour of ashes
blanched   colourless; whitened
bleached   whitened by sunlight or
chemicals
pallid   unusually pale, especially from
illness
pasty   unhealthily pale
sallow   of an unhealthy yellowish
colour
wan   unnaturally pale, especially
from grief or sickness
washed-out   very tired and faded-
looking

waxen   like wax in paleness or
smoothness

*bloodless   deathlike   ghastly
ghostly*

530   paper   n.

charter   official document granting
rights and freedoms
deed   paper that proves and records
an agreement
diploma   document awarding a
qualification, recording examination
success, or completing a course of
study
document   paper giving information
or evidence about something
newsprint   cheap kind of paper used
mostly for newspapers
parchment   heavy paper-like material
made from animal skins
stationery   any writing materials
title   document conferring the legal
right to ownership
warrant   written order signed by an
official of the law
will   written directions made by a
person for the disposal of property
and money after death

certificate   licence   testament

531   parent   n.
father   mother

ancestor   person, especially one living
a long time ago, from whom another
is descended
forbear   person from whom the stated
person is descended
foster-parents   persons who take care
of and bring up a child as their own
godparents   persons who undertake
to see that a child is brought up as
a Christian
guardian   person who legally agrees
to look after another's child,
especially after the parent's death

sire old word for father

step-parent person whom one's father or mother has remarried

532 **part** n.

complement something that completes another; number or quantity needed to fill something

division part of the whole which has been divided

element one of the parts that make up a whole

fraction very small part, piece, or amount

ingredient a particular one of a mixture of things, especially in cooking

majority greatest number or part of a group or class

minority smallest number or part of a group or class

portion share or part of something

remnant small remaining quantity, part, or number of people or things

section distinct part or portion of something

segment any of the parts into which something may be cut or divided

slice thin, flat piece cut from something

snippet small scrap or fragment, especially of something spoken or written

chunk *hunk* *particle* *wedge*

533 **parting** n. (i)

dissociation declaration that one has no connection with something

divorce separation, especially one which is total

rift break in friendly relations between people, or in the unity of a group

separation breaking, coming or being apart

534 **parting** n. (ii)

departure *farewell* *leave-taking*

535 **passable** adj.

acceptable

adequate enough or suitable for the purpose

admissible able or deserving to be considered or allowed

allowable may be permitted

presentable fit to be seen, shown, or heard in public

tolerable fairly good; able to be put up with

middling *so-so*

536 **passive** adj.

inactive

apathetic lacking feeling, interest, or desire to act

inert very slow to move or take action

non-participating not willing to take part or share in an activity

stolid showing little or no emotion or interest

submissive willing to obey humbly and without question

undemonstrative not expressing one's feelings openly

unresisting not opposing or fighting against

unresponsive not reacting warmly by words or feelings

537 **pathetic** adj.

heart-rending very distressing; causing great sorrow

lamentable wretched, regrettable, or distressing

paltry worthless, trivial, contemptible

touching rousing kindly feelings, sympathy, or pity

538 patience n.

diligence steady and attentive hard
 work
doggedness refusal to give up in the
 face of difficulty
endurance ability to withstand pain,
 hardship, or strain
forbearance control of one's feelings,
 showing patience and tolerance
perseverance ability to go on
 steadfastly, especially in something
 difficult or tedious
restraint self-control
self-possession calm and dignified
 control over one's own feelings and
 actions

539 pay v.

advance lend money or pay it before
 the proper time
compensate make a suitable payment
 in return for loss or damage
disburse pay out money
indemnify compensate for loss,
 injury, or expense
refund give back money, especially
 for an unsatisfactory article
remunerate reward or pay a person
 for services rendered

foot the bill

540 people n.
human beings

clan group of families, all originally
 descended from one family
clientele those who use the services of
 professional people, businesses, or
 shops
community group with common
 interests or origins
humankind human beings
kinsmen blood relations, or relations
 by marriage
mankind human race

mortals people (subject to death)
nation large community of people of
 mainly common descent, living in one
 territory under one government
persons individual human beings
 without regard to sex
population total inhabitants of a
 place, district, or country
public members of the community in
 general or a particular section of it
race one of the great divisions of
 mankind with certain inherited
 physical characteristics in common
residents people who live
 permanently in a place
society large group of people with
 shared language, customs and laws

folk

541 perfect adj.
faultless ideal

admirable worthy of being respected
 and looked up to
excellent extremely good; of the
 highest quality
exemplary suitable to be copied;
 serving as a warning
incomparable above comparison;
 matchless; unequalled
unblemished free from flaws or
 defects; spotlessly clean

542 perhaps adv.
maybe possibly
there is a chance that

543 persuade v.
convince

convert cause a person to change his
 attitude or beliefs, usually concerning
 religion
enlist secure as a means of support
induce lead someone to act, usually
 by persuasion

influence   have an effect on someone's character, beliefs, or actions
prevail upon   succeed in persuading or inducing

win over

544   **petty**   adj.

trifling   trivial   unimportant

insignificant   having little or no importance, value, or influence
minor   lesser or secondary in amount, extent, importance, or degree

inessential

545   **picture**   v.

imagine

visualize   form a picture of someone or something in the mind

546   **picture**   n.

collage   artistic composition made by sticking various materials or objects on to a surface
description   account intended to give mental image
engraving   print made from cuts on wood, stone, or metal
etching   picture printed from a metal plate cut with acids
fresco   watercolour picture painted on a wall or ceiling before the plaster is dry
old master   great painter of former times, or one of his pictures
portrait   painting, drawing, or photograph of a real person
representation   artistic likeness or image
still life   painting of lifeless things, such as cut flowers or fruit

sketch   *snapshot*

547   **pink**   adj.

rose

salmon-pink

548   **pitiful**   adj.

pitiable

abject   as low as possible; not deserving respect
beggarly   mean and insufficient; very poor
wretched   poor, miserable, unhappy

549   **plan**   n.

arrangement   agreed preparations for doing something
plot   secret plan by several people to do harm
procedure   set of actions necessary for doing something
programme   definite plan of what is to be done
scheme   clever, sometimes dishonest, plan; orderly planned arrangement
strategy   particular plan for winning success in a particular activity, especially military
tactic   device calculated to achieve a desired result

proposal

550   **pleasant**   adj.

agreeable   pleasing

affable   easy to talk to; polite and friendly
delectable   enjoyable; especially pleasing to the taste
delightful   giving great pleasure
enjoyable   receiving pleasure from
gratifying   satisfying pleasurably

551 pleasure n.

enjoyment

contentment happy and satisfied
with what one has
exhilaration enlivening happiness
fulfilment deep satisfaction of a need
glee triumphant merriment
gratification act or state of being
pleasurably satisfied
rejoicing gladness or great joy,
celebrating some event

gladness happiness

552 plight n.

crisis time of acute difficulty or
danger
dilemma situation in which one must
chose between two evils
extremity highest degree of need,
suffering, misfortune, or danger
predicament difficult, perplexing, or
unpleasant situation
quandary state of perplexity and
doubt

scrape

553 pointless adj.

meaningless purposeless

fatuous foolishly self-satisfied
immaterial of no importance
irrelevant not having any connection
with something
vain without result; useless

absurd

554 poor adj.

destitute lacking the simplest
necessary things of life
impecunious having little or no
money
impoverished made poor

penurious lacking money or means;
mean with money

*badly-off down-and-out needy
penniless poverty-stricken*

555 possible adj.

conceivable able to be imagined or
believed
credible worthy of belief
feasible able to be carried out
practicable able to be successfully
used or acted upon
probable likely to happen or be true

attainable

556 practice n.

convention accepted way of social
behaviour
custom usual way of behaving or
doing something
habit something done frequently and
almost without thinking
procedure way or order of directing
business or accomplishing something
routine regular, ordinary way of
doing things
rule customary or normal state of
things or course of action

observance

557 practised adj.

experienced

knowledgeable well-informed
seasoned experienced through
training and practice
versed possessing a thorough
knowledge or skill

adroit dextrous expert masterful

558 **predict** v.

forecast tell in advance what is likely
to happen
foresee be aware of or realize a thing
beforehand
prophesy foretell future events as if
by divine inspiration

559 **pretty** adj.

appealing pleasing and interesting
attractive having good looks
beautiful giving great pleasure to the
senses or the mind
captivating exciting and capturing
the fancy
dainty small and delicately pretty
elegant graceful, refined, and
dignified in style or appearance
enchanting filling with intense delight
good-looking having a pleasing
appearance
gorgeous strikingly beautiful or
magnificent
graceful very pleasing in movement,
form, or behaviour
handsome fine-looking and well-
proportioned
lovely attractive to both heart and
eye
stunning extremely attractive;
splendid

*engaging exquisite fascinating
ornamental picturesque stylish
winsome*

560 **price** n.

charge cost

duty tax charged on certain goods or
on imports
estimate rough calculation of the cost
of doing something
expense spending of money; amount
of money spent

fare price charged for a passenger to
travel
fee sum payable to a professional
person for advice or services
hire use of a thing for a time for
payment
levy payment imposed or collected
by authority or by force
penalty fine or forfeit imposed as a
punishment
quotation price of something as
known at that time
rent money paid regularly for the use
of property or an object
retail price price of goods sold to
customers for their own use, not for
resale
tariff list of fixed charges, especially
for rooms and meals at a hotel
toll tax or duty paid for the use of a
public road, bridge, or harbour
wholesale price price of goods sold in
large quantities for resale

forfeit valuation

561 **pride** n.

arrogance exaggerated and self-
important pride
bumptiousness offensive and self-
assertive conceit
conceit too high an opinion of one's
own abilities and value
haughtiness high and mighty
manner; looking down on others
vanity far too proud of one's
appearance, possessions, or
achievements

*complacence presumption self-
importance self-satisfaction*

562 **prisoner** n.

captive person or animal taken
prisoner and/or unable to escape

convict   person found guilty of a crime and sent to prison
jailbird   person who has spent a lot of time in prison
trusty   prisoner who is granted special privileges because of continous good behaviour

563   private   adj.

confidential   trusted with private matters; to be kept secret
off-the-record   not to be written down in the notes of the meeting
restricted   limited to selected persons
unofficial   not yet said to be true by those in charge

564   prize   n. (i)

award   something that is given, especially on the basis of merit or need
jackpot   largest amount of money to be won in a game of chance
lottery   arrangement in which people buy tickets, a few of which are picked by chance to win prizes
sweepstake   form of betting in which the winners gain all the money paid in
trophy   object given as a prize or token of victory
windfall   unexpectedly lucky gift or good fortune

winnings

565   prize   n. (ii)

booty   goods stolen by thieves or taken by a victorious army
loot   goods stolen, as in wartime or during riots
plunder   valuables, goods, or sacred items taken by force
seizure   goods taken forcibly
spoils   anything of value seized by violence, especially in war

566   probably   adv.

likely

apparently   doubtless
in all likelihood

567   procession   n.

cavalcade   procession of people on horseback, in carriages, and in cars
column   long narrow formation of troops, people, or vehicles
cortège   funeral procession or procession of attendants
file   line of people or things one behind the other
march past   ceremonial march past a saluting-point
motorcade   procession of cars
parade   formal assembly of troops for inspection; procession of people or things, especially in a display or exhibition
retinue   number of attendants accompanying an important person
train   number of people or animals moving in a line

march

568   profit   n.

gain

advantage   more favourable position; benefit or profit
benefit   something helpful, favourable, or profitable
income   money received regularly for work, or as interest
interest   money paid for the use of money lent
return   money gained from an investment, transaction, or venture
revenue   annual amount of money received by a country from taxes
yield   amount produced; quantity obtained

recompense

569 promptly adv.

punctually

briskly doing what is required
without undue delay
expediently suitable to the
circumstances
timely happening or coming at just
the right moment

immediately unhesitatingly

570 proof n.

confirmation act of establishing
proof of the truth of something
corroboration supporting or
strengthening fact or opinion by
fresh information
evidence anything that establishes a
fact, or gives reason for believing
something
ratification formal approval or
consent
validation declaration of legal
acceptability

documentation

571 proper adj.

correct fitting

becoming suitable
decent conforming to the accepted
standards of what is respectable
decorous correct in manners and
behaviour
seemly in accordance with accepted
standards of good taste

572 proud adj.

arrogant too proud and self-
important
cocksure too sure of oneself
conceited valuing oneself too highly
haughty disdainful; having or
showing arrogance

patronizing treating others as less
important or of less worth than
oneself
self-assertive pushing forward one's
own abilities or claims
self-important having too high an
opinion of one's own importance
supercilious scornful and high and
mighty in manner

big-headed condescending
disdainful pompous snobbish

573 proverb n.

adage traditional saying accepted by
many as true
aphorism short wise saying
axiom accepted general truth or
principle
epigram short witty saying or poem
maxim rule for good and sensible
behaviour
platitude commonplace remark,
especially one uttered solemnly as if
it were new
truism statement of something that is
obviously or indisputably true

574 pull v.

drag pull along the ground with
effort or difficulty
draw pull a cart or sledge
tow pull along behind by a rope or
chain
tug pull suddenly and strongly
yank make a sudden, sharp pull

575 pure adj.

immaculate without spot or stain
unalloyed not weakened or spoiled,
especially by unpleasant feelings
uncontaminated not mixed with dirty
or poisonous matter

chaste stainless wholesome

576 push v.

impel send, drive, or push forward
jog shake slightly with a jerk or push
jolt dislodge or shake with a sudden jerk
jostle knock or push roughly, especially when in a crowd
nudge push slightly or gradually
poke push sharply with the end of a finger or stick
propel drive or cause to move forward
shove push roughly
trundle roll along; move along heavily on a wheel or wheels

press forward   *shoulder through*
squeeze through

577 put v.

place

deposit set down carefully or in its proper place
drop fall by force of gravity from not being held
lay place or put on a surface or in a certain position
locate fix or set in a certain place
plant set in place; put seeds or plants in the ground
plonk place or drop down with a hollow sound
pose sit, stand, or be put in a particular position
position put in a suitable place for a particular purpose
situate allot a site to
station place or stand in a position already decided

park

578 puzzle n.

conundrum puzzling question or problem

enigma person, thing, or situation that is mysterious and puzzling
mystery something that remains unexplained or secret
problem something difficult to deal with or understand
riddle difficult and amusing question to which one must guess the answer

perplexity

579 qualm n.

misgiving

compunction pricking of conscience; slight regret
pang painful emotion
remorse deep regret for having done wrong
scruple doubt or hesitation about what is right in a certain situation
self-reproach blaming oneself for a fault or offence

580 quarrel n.

bickering quarrelling constantly about unimportant things
brawl noisy quarrel, usually including fighting
controversy argument about something over which there is much disagreement
disagreement having different opinions and failing to agree
discord lack of agreement, usually causing conflict or argument
dissension disagreement leading to a quarrel
squabble childish, noisy quarrel about unimportant things
wrangle angry, noisy argument

feud   *riot*   *vendetta*

581 quell v.

subdue suppress

crush defeat or subdue completely
pacify restore to peace and order
put down suppress by force or
  authority
subjugate conquer or take power
  over
vanquish defeat completely

conquer defeat stamp out

582 quench v.

damp down heap ashes on a fire to
  make it burn more slowly
extinguish put out completely
satisfy put an end to a demand or
  craving by giving what is required
smother put out or reduce a fire by
  keeping out air
stifle prevent from happening or
  continuing

583 question n.

enquiry request for information
issue important topic for discussion
leading question question formed so
  that it suggests the answer
loaded question question that
  contains a hidden trap
query question expressing doubt or
  objection

doubt uncertainty

584 quick adj.

fast speedy

sudden happening or done
  unexpectedly or without warning
swift moving or able to move fast

cursory fleet of foot

585 quiet adj.

hushed still and silent
muted deadened or muffled in sound
subdued made quieter or less intense

peaceable soundless

586 quite adv. (i)

*completely entirely fully really
truly*

quite adv. (ii)

rather somewhat

587 rabble n.

mob

dregs worst and useless part
hoi polloi common people; the
  masses
proletariat class of unskilled wage
  earners
scum worthless, evil people

*outcasts ragtag and bobtail
riff-raff*

588 rain n.

deluge great flood; very heavy fall of
  rain
downpour heavy, continuous fall of
  rain for a short period
drizzle very fine, light rain
shower brief fall of rain or snow
torrent violently rushing streams of
  water

589 random adj.

aimless without direction
arbitrary based on choice or impulse,
  not on reason
casual happening by chance; made or
  done without forethought

desultory   passing from one thing to
  another without purpose or method
haphazard   careless; slipshod
unmethodical   without order or
  system

chance   unconsidered

590   **rank**   adj. (i)

exuberant   growing in great
  abundance and profusion
luxuriant   growing thickly, richly,
  and strongly
overgrown   having grown too much
  or too fast

rank   adj. (ii)

foul-smelling   foul-tasting   offensive

591   **rash**   adj.

heedless   reckless

foolhardy   boldly but rashly taking
  unnecessary risks
hasty   hurried; speedy
impetuous   acting on impulse too
  hastily and thoughtlessly
incautious   not careful to pay the
  necessary attention
indiscreet   unwisely revealing secrets
  or confidences
injudicious   showing lack of good
  judgement
precipitate   violently hurried

harum-scarum   hot-headed
overbold   uncontrolled   unwary

592   **rather**   adv.

after a fashion   more exactly
more truly   somewhat   sooner
to a certain extent

593   **reach**   v. (i)

arrive at

communicate   connect one thing with
  another; pass on or make known

attain   set foot on

reach   v. (ii)

stretch out

extend   stretch or continue
border on   be next to

594   **read**   v.

peruse   read or examine with care
revise   read again, altering,
  correcting, or improving
scan   look at quickly without careful
  reading
skim   read quickly, noting only the
  chief points
study   spend time in learning or
  considering carefully

dip into   glance over   pore over
thumb through

595   **ready**   adj.

prepared

available   ready or able to be
  obtained or used
equipped   supplied with what is
  necessary
furnished   provided with what is
  necessary for a special purpose
mature   fully grown or developed
primed   fully prepared for action or
  use
ripe   ready to be picked and eaten or
  used

liable to   well-provided

596 real adj.

genuine

actual existing in fact; real
authentic known to be what it is
claimed to be
bona fide genuine, without fraud
realistic based on facts, not on ideas
or illusions
tangible clear and definite, not
imaginary
unfeigned not pretending or false
valid well-grounded in truth

597 really adv.

actually   genuinely   in fact
in reality   positively   truly
unquestionably

598 reasonable adj.

equitable fair and just
logical correctly reasoned
plausible seeming to be reasonable or
probable, but not proved
pragmatic treating things from a
practical point of view
rational well-reasoned and sensible
sensible having good sense

commonsensical   well-founded

599 rebuke v.

berate scold harshly
chide find fault with in a nagging
way
lecture give a long, solemn scolding
reprehend find fault with; criticize
reprimand give a severe, official
scolding
reprove express disapproval of a
fault or error
upbraid find fault with angrily and
harshly

dress down   haul over the coals
read the riot act

600 recover v. (i)

regain

recall take back; call to return from a
place
recapture capture a person or thing
that has escaped or been lost to an
enemy
reclaim demand as the rightful
owner; recover possession of
recoup recover what one has lost or
its equivalent
repossess get back possession
retrieve find and bring back; put
right a mistake, loss, or defeat

recover v. (ii)

recuperate get better from being ill

convalesce   pull through

601 red adj.

cardinal deep scarlet
carmine vivid red colour sometimes
with purplish tinge
cerise light clear red
cherry bright red colour of a ripe
cherry
cochineal bright red colouring matter
for food
crimson vivid red
florid having a red or flushed
complexion
magenta deep purplish-red
maroon dark red to purplish-red
ruby colour of a deep red transparent
precious stone
ruddy face with a fresh, healthy
reddish colour
rufous reddish brown
sanguine blood-red; ruddy in
appearance
scarlet vivid red colour, sometimes
with an orange tinge

bloodshot   fiery

602 refresh v.

brace freshen or fill with energy
reanimate fill with new strength or courage
rejuvenate make or become young again
renew make as good as new; replace
restore bring back to its original state
resuscitate restore to consciousness
revive bring or be brought back to life, consciousness, or strength

energize *revitalize*

603 region n.

department specialized division of a government or large business
district part of a country, city, county, or area
locale place or area in which certain events take place
province one of the main divisions of some countries for purposes of government control
territory land under the control of a ruler, state or city
zone division or area marked off from others

604 regret v.

bemoan be very sorry for or over something
bewail express great sorrow over a person or thing
grieve feel intense sorrow or distress, especially at someone's death
lament feel or express remorse or regret
miss feel the lack or loss of
rue repent or regret

apologize *repent*

605 regular adj. (i)

accustomed *customary* *everyday*
habitual *normal* *standard* *usual*

606 regular adj. (ii)

even unvarying, level
methodical orderly and very careful
permanent meant to last for a long time
regulated something adjusted so that it works correctly
symmetrical having balanced proportions
systematic based on a regular plan or fixed method
uniform not varying

balanced *orderly* *steady*

607 reliable adj.

dependable trustworthy

608 remarkable adj.

imposing grand and impressive
impressive arousing particular admiration and approval
singular uncommon; of unusual quality
striking sure to be noticed

astonishing *astounding*

609 remember v.

commemorate keep in the memory by means of a celebration or ceremony
memorize learn so as to remember
recall bring back to mind
recollect call something to mind; remember
recognize know again someone or something one has met before
remind cause to remember or think of something
reminisce talk pleasantly about the past

610 remiss adj.

negligent

dilatory slow in doing something;
  causing delay purposely
improvident not providing for future
  needs
perfunctory done as a duty or routine
  but without much care
slipshod done as a duty or routine
  but without much care or interest

careless neglectful slapdash

611 repeat v.

reiterate

paraphrase express something
  written or said in different words
recapitulate state again the main
  points of what has been said or
  discussed
recite say aloud from memory,
  especially before an audience
regurgitate bring up again
rehearse learn and practise for later
  performance; say over again
rephrase express in other words,
  especially more clearly
restate say again, perhaps in different
  words
retell say again
reword change the wording of

echo parrot reproduce

612 reputation n.

estimation judgement or opinion of a
  person's worth
face appearance or pretence
name outward appearance or form,
  not necessarily the truth
repute what is said or thought to be
  true about someone
standing position in society
status person's position or rank in
  relation to others

admiration

613 rescue v.

save

deliver set free
free set at liberty; release
liberate set free, especially from
  control by an authority that is
  considered to be oppressive
ransom obtain the release of a
  captive in return for payment

614 resentful adj.

embittered filled with painful and
  bitter feelings
hostile opposed to; very unfriendly
incensed enraged; made very angry
piqued irritated because of wounded
  pride
provoked angrily roused to action

antagonistic revengeful

615 resourceful adj.

astute quick at seeing how to gain an
  advantage
creative producing new and original
  ideas or things
quick-witted quick to understand
  and act

616 restless adj.

uneasy unsettled

fidgety nervous and restless
fretful constantly worrying or crying
highly-strung excitable and easily
  upset
restive restless and resisting control
  because made impatient by delay or
  restraint

*edgy itchy jumpy keyed up
on tenterhooks*

617 return v.

come back   go back

backtrack   go back over the same path
ebb   flow away from shore; become lower or weaker
reappear   come into sight or view again
recede   go or shrink back from a certain point
reciprocate   give something in return for something felt, done, or given
reoccur   happen again
restore   give or put back
retreat   move back, especially when forced to
reverse   move in the opposite direction
wane   grow smaller in size; decrease in vigour, strength, or importance

618 reveal v.

disclose   make known

blab   let out a secret
divulge   make known something private or secret
impart   give or make known information
inform   give information; tell facts
leak   allow secret or confidential information to escape
proclaim   make known publicly or officially
publish   make generally known; announce formally
release   allow a news story to be printed
ventilate   express an opinion publicly so that others may consider and discuss it

announce   uncover   unmask

619 review v.

reconsider   re-examine

criticize   make judgements about the good and bad points
summarize   state briefly the main points of
sum up   consider and judge quickly

620 revise v.

correct   go over

amend   correct errors; change for the better
edit   prepare written material for publication
emend   alter something written to remove mistakes
redraft   prepare a second rough version of something written
rework   use again in altered form
rewrite   write again in a different way
update   bring up to date

621 rhythm n.

beat   regular repeated sound
cadence   pattern in sound
flow   steady, smooth movement in sound
lilt   light, pleasant pattern of rising and falling sound
pulse   short, regular single beat
tempo   speed at which music is played

622 rich adj.

moneyed   wealthy

affluent   having plenty of money or other possessions
flush   well-supplied with money at that moment
lavish   generous or wasteful with money
opulent   having or indicating great wealth
sumptuous   splendid and costly-looking

in clover   well-heeled   well-to-do

623 river n.

beck   brook   cascade   cataract
rapids   reach   rill   rivulet   runnel
sluice   stream   tributary

624 road n.

avenue   wide street or road, often
lined with trees
boulevard   wide, usually tree-lined,
road in a city
bypass   road taking traffic round a
congested area
drive   private road leading to a house
highroad   main road
highway   main route for any form of
transport
street   public road in a town or village
with houses on one or both sides
thoroughfare   road for public traffic

motorway

625 rob v.

burgle   break into a building and steal
embezzle   take wrongfully, for one's
own use, money or property placed
in one's care
misappropriate   take dishonestly,
especially for one's own use
peculate   take wrongfully, for one's
own use, money placed in one's care
pilfer   steal small things or in small
quantities
plunder   seize goods unlawfully or by
force
purloin   take something dishonestly
steal   take another person's property
without right or permission
thieve   steal, especially stealthily and
without violence

knock off   nick   pinch   shoplift
swipe

626 rope n.

cable   thick, heavy, strong rope, wire,
or chain
cordage   lines and rigging of a vessel
guy   rope or chain used to keep
something steady or secured
halyard   rope for raising or lowering a
rope, flag, or sail
hawser   heavy rope or cable for
mooring or towing a ship
painter   light rope fastened to the bow
of a small boat for tying it up
rigging   ropes used to support masts
and set or work the sails on a ship
tackle   set of ropes and pulleys for
lifting weights, or working a ship's
sails

627 rot v.

decay   go or cause to go bad
decompose   break down by bacteria
or fungi
fester   make or become infected and
filled with pus
moulder   decay slowly into dust
perish   lose or cause to lose its normal
qualities
putrefy   rot with a foul smell

628 rotten adj. (i)

abominable   very bad or unpleasant
contemptible   deserving contempt;
worthless
despicable   deserving to be regarded
as worthless
detestable   hateful
disgusting   sickening, distasteful, or
objectionable
loathsome   filling with hatred and
disgust

rotten adj. (ii)

decayed   decomposed   mouldy

putrid   having rotted or decayed

629 row n.

argument   dispute   quarrel   wrangle

630 rub v.

buff   polish with something soft
burnish   polish with something hard and smooth, especially metal
chafe   make or become sore from rubbing
grate   shred into small pieces by rubbing against a jagged surface
knead   press and stretch with the hands to make soft
massage   press and rub the body to lessen pain or stiffness
polish   make, or become, smooth and glossy by rubbing
rasp   scrape with a coarse file
scour   clean a surface by hard rubbing with a rough material
scrub   rub hard with a stiff brush
smooth   remove roughnesses to make an even surface

631 rude adj.

discourteous   impolite   unmannerly

brusque   abrupt and rather impolite
curt   rudely short in speech and manner
disparaging   speaking of in a slighting way; belittling
disrespectful   treating someone as not worthy of polite consideration
impertinent   cheeky in speech and behaviour
impudent   shamelessly bold
insolent   showing disrespectful rudeness
insulting   speaking or acting in a way that hurts the feelings or pride of a person and rouses their anger
pert   saucy and forward, often in an amusing way
uncivil   not polite or obliging

uncouth   ill-mannered; awkward and clumsy in manner
vulgar   behaving in a very rude and low way

boorish   coarse   indecent   loutish

632 sad adj.

unhappy

crestfallen   downcast; very disappointed at failure
dejected   in low spirits
depressed   sad and discouraged
despondent   feeling a complete loss of hope
miserable   feeling very unhappy, uneasy, or uncomfortable
sorrowful   feeling very unhappy over loss or wrongdoing

blue   down-hearted   down-in-the-dumps   heavy-hearted   woe-begone

633 safe adj.

secure

defended   protected against attack
guarded   kept safe, especially by watching for danger
immune   free from; not susceptible to
impregnable   which cannot be entered or conquered by attack, especially a fortress
invulnerable   that cannot be harmed
protected   kept from harm or injury, especially by covering
sheltered   shielded from harm
unassailable   able to withstand violent and persistent attack

634 salty adj.

briny   full of salt (of water)
brackish   slightly salty (of water)
saline   of, concerned with, consisting of, or containing common salt

piquant

635 same adj.
identical

comparable able to be examined or judged against another
corresponding be in agreement with
duplicate exactly like another thing
equivalent equal in amount, force or value
matching like or suitable for use with something else
similar partly or almost the same
synonymous equal or nearly equal in meaning; closely associated with

self-same unchanging

636 sarcastic adj.

derisive making fun of in a mocking way
ironic bitterly funny
jeering laughing or shouting at rudely
sardonic humorous in a grim or sarcastic way
taunting making scornful remarks or criticism in order to provoke

637 savage adj.
fierce untamed

barbarous brutal or very cruel; uncivilized
cruel liking to cause pain or suffering
primitive simple or crude
uncivilized behaving in a rough and crude way

diabolical fiendish

638 save v. (i)

extricate set free from something that is difficult to escape from
rescue save or bring away from attack, capture, or danger
salvage rescue goods or property from fire or shipwreck

639 save v. (ii)

hoard save and store away
husband save carefully or make the best use of
reserve put aside for a later occasion or for special use
scrape live with no more than the barely necessary money
scrimp save money slowly and with difficulty, especially by living poorly
stockpile keep adding to a stock of goods or materials kept in reserve
withhold keep back on purpose

economize

640 say v.

affirm state as a fact
allege state without being able to prove
announce make known publicly
articulate say or speak distinctly
assert state forcefully
convey make known as an idea or meaning
declare state firmly
express put a thought, feeling, opinion, or fact into words
hint suggest indirectly
mouth say publicly something insincerely; form words with the lips without speaking them aloud
pronounce utter a sound distinctly or in a certain way; declare officially
remark comment on; notice
snap speak with sudden irritation
tell make something known in words

enunciate utter whisper

641 scarcely adv.
barely hardly not quite only just

642   scare   n.

alarm   fright

horror   feeling of great shock and fear
jitters   nervousness before an event
panic   sudden uncontrollable fear
phobia   lasting out-of-the-ordinary
fear or dread of something
shock   a sudden and violent mental or
physical impression
terror   very great fear, panic, or dread

643   scent   n.

aroma   distinctive, usually pleasant,
smell
attar   pleasant-smelling oil obtained
from flowers
bouquet   smell of wine
essence   liquid perfume
fragrance   sweet and pleasant smell
incense   substance that produces a
sweet smell when burning
odour   characteristic scent or smell
perfume   fragrant liquid for giving a
pleasant smell, especially to the body
redolence   strong smell
trail   scent or track followed in
hunting

644   scold   v.

admonish   tell off or warn gently
castigate   punish severely in order to
correct
chastise · punish severely by beating
chide   tell off, but not severely
rebuke   give a short official scolding
reprimand   give a severe official
scolding
reprove   blame or scold for a fault or
error
upbraid   find fault with angrily

645   scratch   v.

abrade   scrape or wear away by
rubbing

bark   scrape the skin off accidently
graze   scrape the skin lightly
scrape   hurt or damage a surface by
rubbing roughly
scuff   make a rough mark or marks on
a surface

646   scream   v.

screech   cry out on a very high, sharp
note
shriek   cry out with a shrill, piercing
sound
squall   cry noisily
squawk   make a loud, harsh cry
squeal   utter a long, shrill cry or
sound
yelp   make a short, sharp, high cry, as
of pain or excitement

647   sea   n.

high seas   open seas not under any
country's control
main   poetic word for the open ocean
ocean   mass of water that covers most
of the earth

briny   *Davy Jones's locker*   *the drink*

648   seat   n.

bench   long seat for two or more
people
box   compartment with seats for
several persons in a theatre
chair   movable seat, with a back, for
one person
couch   long upholstered seat, usually
with a back and arms
cushion   bag filled with a soft
substance on which a person can sit
hassock   thick firm cushion for
kneeling on in church
pew   long bench with a back for
sitting on in church

settle   long wooden seat with a high
solid back and a bottom part which is
a chest
sofa   long upholstered seat with a
back and raised ends or arms
squab   stuffed seat or cushion,
especially as part of a car seat
stall   one of the set of seats in the part
of a theatre nearest to the stage
stool   seat without a supporting part
for one's back or arms

649   see   v.

descry   notice something far off
discern   recognize or perceive clearly
espy   catch sight of
notice   become aware of
perceive   see or notice
sight   get a view of, especially after a
time of looking
spot   watch for and take note of

650   seedy   adj.

run-down   scruffy   shabby

degraded   reduced in worth;
disgraced or dishonoured
down-at-heel   wearing shoes with
worn-down heels and old well-worn
clothes
mangy   very untidy and careless in
appearance
sleazy   dirty, cheap and poor-looking
squalid   dirty and unpleasant,
especially because of neglect or
poverty

651   seek   v.

look for   search for

ransack   search thoroughly or
roughly
rummage   turn things over while
trying to find something

inquire for   nose out

652   seldom   adv.

hardly ever   infrequently
not often   once in a while
rarely   scarcely ever

653   selfish   adj.

egotistic   talking and thinking too
much about one's own importance
self-centred   interested only in oneself
self-indulgent   giving way too easily
to one's own desires for pleasure or
comfort
self-seeking   working only for one's
own advantage

654   send   v.

consign   hand over or deliver
formally; give into someone's care
deliver   carry and distribute things to
several places; hand over, transfer, or
surrender
forward   send on to a new address or
to a customer
post   put a letter etc. into a post office
or post-box for sending on
remit   send money by post
ship   send by ship; put or take on
board a ship for taking somewhere

broadcast   radio   telegraph   televise

655   serious   adj.

earnest

acute   coming quickly to a dangerous
condition
critical   very serious; of or at a crisis
important   having or able to have a
great effect
meditative   thinking seriously or
deeply
reflective   thoughtful

menacing   touch-and-go

656 shake v.

chatter make a repeated clicking sound

oscillate move to and fro like a pendulum

quake shake or tremble from fear or unsteadiness

rattle make or cause to make a series of short, sharp, hard sounds

shiver tremble slightly from cold or fear

shudder shake uncontrollably for a moment from fear, cold, or strong dislike

vibrate move unceasingly to and fro, especially rapidly

quiver *tremble* *twitch*

657 shameful adj.

belittling implying that something is unimportant or of little value

discreditable unworthy; damaging a good reputation

disgraceful causing loss of respect

dishonourable lacking honesty and principles

humiliating causing a feeling of shame or disgrace

ignoble not noble or honourable in character, aims, or purpose

ignominious shameful to one's pride

improper not seemly or fitting

vile extremely disgusting

658 shine v.

blaze burn with a bright flame

dazzle make unable to see clearly because of too much bright light

flare burn with a sudden irregular flame for a short time

flash give out a sudden bright light

flicker burn or shine unsteadily

glare shine with a strong, unpleasant light

gleam give out a ray of soft light

glimmer give a very faint, unsteady light

glint give out small flashes of light

glisten shine from or as if from a wet surface

glitter shine brightly with flashing points of light

glow send out light and heat without flame

radiate send out light or heat in rays

scintillate give off sparks

shimmer shine with a soft, trembling light

sparkle shine with bright points of light

twinkle shine with an unsteady light that quickly changes from bright to faint and keeps doing this

659 ship n.

boat small ship

ferry boat that carries people and things across a river or other narrow stretch of water

freighter ship or aircraft for carrying goods

liner large passenger ship

merchantman ship carrying goods to be sold wholesale

schooner fast sailing-ship with two or sometimes more masts

steamer large non-naval ship driven by steam power

tanker ship, aircraft, or vehicle for carrying oil or other liquid in bulk

whaler ship engaged in hunting whales

vessel

660 shop n.

boutique small shop selling clothes of the latest fashion

department store large shop divided into separate departments in which different goods are sold *retail store* shop selling goods to customers for their own use, not for resale

supermarket large self-service shop selling groceries and household goods

wholesale store large building selling goods in large quantities for resale

workshop room or building in which manual work or manufacture is carried out

661 shore n.

beach shore between high and low water mark with sand or water-worn pebbles; land by a lake or river used for swimming and sunbathing

coast land next to the sea

foreshore area along the edge of the sea and where there is grass or buildings

seaboard part of a country along a sea-coast

seashore land along the edge of the sea

seaside sea-coast, especially as a place for holidays

strand shore or beach

waterside edge of a river, lake, or sea

662 shortly adv. (i)

before long   briefly   by and by   soon

shortly adv. (ii)

concisely   curtly   gruffly

663 shout v.

*bellow   call out   catcall   cry
cry out   holler   whoop   yell*

664 show v.

bring out cause to appear; show clearly

demonstrate show the value or use of

display arrange a thing so that it can be seen

exhibit present for the public to see

indicate point out

present offer or bring to someone's notice

unveil uncover; make publicly known

authenticate

665 shy adj.

bashful   retiring

diffident hesitating to put oneself or one's ideas forward

reserved not liking to talk about oneself or show one's feelings

reticent inclined to be silent; reserved in speech

self-conscious nervous and uncomfortable about oneself as seen by others

shrinking unwilling to do something because of shame or dislike

withdrawn unsociable; unusually reserved

666 silly adj.

absurd   foolish   ridiculous

asinine acting like a stupid donkey

farcical happening as in a humorous play

fatuous foolish in a self-satisfied way

frivolous unable to take important matters seriously

idiotic senseless; very stupid

inane empty of meaning; senseless

ludicrous causing laughter and ridicule

nonsensical not making sense

outrageous shocking; exceeding greatly what is moderate or reasonable
preposterous completely unreasonable or improbable
unwise foolish and thoughtless

childish *comical* *laughable* *unreasonable*

667 **sing** v.

chant sing or recite a psalm or prayer
croon sing gently in a low, soft voice
hymn sing praises to God or another sacred being
intone say a poem or prayer in a level voice
serenade sing or play in the open air at night, especially to one's lover
trill sing briefly or lightly as a bird
vocalize express with or use the voice
warble sing with trills, runs, and other fancy additions

chirp *hum* *pipe*

668 **sit** v.

bestride have or put a leg on either side of
crouch lower the body close to the ground by bending knees and back
hunker down sit on one's heels
lounge stand or sit in a leaning, lazy manner
perch rest or place on something narrow or high
squat crouch with knees drawn up closely
straddle sit or stand across a thing with the legs wide apart

669 **size** n.

bulk mass, volume
dimensions length, breadth and height

magnitude greatness of size or importance
proportions measurements and shape as they relate to one another
volume amount of space that a three-dimensional thing occupies or contains; strength or power of sound

measurements

670 **sketchy** adj.

brief in as few words as possible
preliminary coming before a main action or event
preparatory done in order to get ready for something
provisional arranged or agreed upon for the time being, but possibly to be altered later
superficial lacking in thoroughness and care

crude *incomplete*

671 **skill** n.

adeptness high degree of skill
competence ability to do satisfactorily what is needed
dexterity skill in handling things
efficiency satisfactory results produced with little waste or effort
expertise special skill, knowledge, or judgement
handiness cleverness with one's hands
know-how practical skill or knowledge in a particular activity

adroitness *facility* *faculty* *knack*

·672 **sleep** v.

catnap take a very short, light sleep
doze sleep lightly
drowse be half asleep
nap have a short sleep during the day
slumber sleep peacefully

snooze   take a short, light sleep during the day

nod off   take a siesta

673   **slogan**   n.

catchphrase   a few words which become popular for a time and used by everybody
motto   short sentence expressing the aims and ideals of a family, country, or institution; verse or riddle inside a paper cracker

674   **slow**   adj. (i)

dawdling   walking slowly and idly; wasting time
deliberate   unhurried and careful
lagging   failing to keep up with others
leisurely   relaxed without hurry
plodding   working at a slow but steady rate
unhurried   done with ample time and without haste

675   **slow**   adj. (ii)

backward   having made less than normal progress
dense   stupid
doltish   slow-thinking and foolish
dull   slow in understanding
obtuse   mentally slow or emotionally insensitive
simple   feeble-minded
unintelligent   without much ability to reason or understand

dull-witted   slow-witted   stupid thick

676   **sly**   adj.

artful   crafty   cunning   wily

cagey   cautious about giving information; secretive

shady   of very doubtful honesty or character
slippery   not to be trusted or relied upon

sneaky

677   **small**   adj.

little

diminutive   remarkably small
dwarfed   much below the average height or size
miniature   greatly reduced in size; made or represented on a small scale
minute   extremely small
pint-sized   very small
short   measuring little from end to end in space or time; of small stature
tiny   very small

678   **smelly**   adj.

fetid   having a stale, sickening, decaying smell
malodorous   having a bad smell
nauseating   having a sickening or disgusting smell
noisome   offensively smelly
putrid   very decayed and bad smelling
rank   highly offensive and disagreeable

foul-smelling   stinking

679   **smile**   v.

beam   smile brightly and happily
grimace   twist the face in pain or disgust, or to cause amusement
grin   smile broadly showing the teeth
simper   smile in a silly, unnatural way
smirk   smile in a false or too self-satisfied way

680 smooth adj.

burnished shiny and smooth;
  polished by rubbing
glossy smooth and reflecting the light
sleek smooth and well-cared for in
  appearance

*glassy icy oily polished satiny
silky*

681 so adv. (i)
very

so conj. (ii)
therefore thus

682 soft adj.

flabby too soft and limp
flaccid hanging loose or wrinkled
pliable bending easily without
  breaking
pliant supple

*crumbly doughy jelly-like limp
over-ripe pulpy spongy squashy
squishy*

683 solid adj.

congealed semi-solid instead of liquid
crystallized clear, definite, and solid
  in form
firm hard, solid structure
impenetrable unable to be gone into
  or through
impermeable which substances,
  especially liquids, cannot get
  through
insoluble unable to be dissolved
stable not easily moved or changed

hard

684 sometime adj.
erstwhile former late

685 sometimes adv.

at times now and again
occasionally on occasion

686 somewhat adv.

fairly in part rather
to some extent

687 song n.

air simple tune for singing or playing
anthem religious song sung in church
  by a choir
ballad song or poem that tells a story,
  usually with a chorus
chant psalm or prayer sung or recited
descant tune sung or played, usually
  higher, in accompaniment to the main
  tune
ditty short, simple song
folk-song song handed down by
  word of mouth; modern imitation of
  this
lyric words of a song; short poem
melody song or tune; clearly
  recognizable tune in a larger
  arrangement of notes
round part-song in which the voices
  follow each other at equal intervals
  at the same pitch
shanty song formerly sung by sailors
  in time to their work
spiritual religious folk-song, sung
  originally by American negroes
tune number of musical notes, one
  after the other, that produce a
  pleasing pattern of sounds

688 soon adv.
presently shortly

ere long forthwith

689 sore adj.

aching having a continuous, dull pain
burning having a very hot feeling
inflamed red and swollen because hurt or diseased
painful suffering great discomfort
raw having the surface of the skin rubbed off
sensitive easily hurt
smarting stinging pain that lasts for some time
stinging feeling a sudden, sharp pain
tender painful when touched; sensitive

690 sound n.

blare harsh, loud sound
blast sudden loud sound as of a trumpet or car horn
chime sound made by a set of bells
clank short, loud sound of metal striking metal
clatter number of rapid short knocks
clink thin, sharp sound like glasses striking together
creak harsh squeak like that of an unoiled hinge
grate harsh noise made by rubbing
groan long, deep sound caused by the movement of wood or metal parts heavily loaded
howl long, loud wailing cry of a dog; similar noise made by a strong wind or an electrical amplifier
knell sound of a bell tolled solemnly after a death or at a funeral
moan low, mournful sound
peal loud ringing of bells or burst of thunder
rasp harsh, grating sound
ring loud, clear sound like a bell
roar deep, loud, continuing sound like that made by a lion
rumble deep, heavy, rolling sound
tinkle short, light, metallic sounds

toll sound of a bell ringing slowly and repeatedly

691 sour adj.

curdled milk separated into soft, thick lumps and clear liquid
rancid tasting or smelling like stale fat

acid tart vinegary

692 space n.

area expanse

capaciousness ability to hold a lot
capacity amount that something can hold
immensity enormous expanse
interval space between two objects or moments in time
leeway room for free movement within limits
spaciousness great amount of room
vastness very great in area or size

acreage elbow-room

693 special adj.

distinctive not commonly found elsewhere
memorable worth remembering; noticeable
outstanding exceptionally good; better than others
pre-eminent above all others
rare very uncommon; seldom found or occurring
select picked out as best or most suitable

*extraordinary noteworthy
out-of-the-ordinary*

694 spectator n.

*beholder bystander eye-witness
observer onlooker*

695 speechless adj.

dumbfounded unable to speak because of surprise or lack of understanding
dumbstruck temporarily deprived of speech through shock or surprise
inarticulate unable to express oneself clearly
non-plussed not knowing what to think or do

tongue-tied

696 speed n.

rapidity swiftness

alacrity prompt and eager readiness
dispatch speed and effectiveness of action
velocity rate of movement, especially in a given direction

697 spend v.

pay out

disburse pay out money
expend use up or spend
lay out spend money for a special purpose
splurge spend money freely and with great show
squander spend foolishly and wastefully

dish out fork out shell out

698 spite n.

animosity powerful and active dislike or hostility
antagonism active opposition or hatred between people or groups
ill will unkind feeling
malevolence evil feeling towards others
malice wish or intention to harm others

pique feeling of hurt pride
venom strong, bitter feeling; hatred

envy jealousy resentment

699 spoil v. (i)

damage harm impair

deface spoil by writing or making marks on
disfigure spoil the appearance
mar damage or spoil
tarnish make or become dull or discoloured
vandalize damage property wilfully or maliciously

ruin

700 spoil v. (ii)

coddle give way too much to the desires of someone
dote on show too much fondness for
indulge allow people to have what they wish
pamper treat too kindly
pervert lead astray from right behaviour or beliefs

overprotect

701 stale adj.

musty smelling unpleasantly old
wilted limp and drooping
withered shrivelled; without freshness or vitality

mouldy tasteless

702 stare v.

eye look at carefully, warily, or with desire
gape stare with open mouth in surprise or wonder
glare stare angrily or fiercely

goggle   stare stupidly or fixedly, as in astonishment
watch   keep one's eyes fixed on

703   **stay**   v.

remain

abide   remain; dwell
endure   remain in existence; last
lodge   stay, usually for a short time, and paying rent
sojourn   live for a time in a place
survive   live after the death of another

704   **stealthy**   adj.

clandestine   done secretly, often for an unlawful reason
covert   concealed or secret
furtive   sly and secretive
surreptitious   done or gained in secret, or by dishonest means
undercover   done or acting in secret

705   **steep**   adj.

abrupt   very steep or sudden
precipitous   dangerously steep like the edge of a cliff
sheer   straight up or down with no slope

706   **steep**   v.

soak

brew   make beer; make tea ready for drinking
immerse   put completely into water
marinate   steep meat or fish in seasoned flavoured liquid before cooking
pickle   preserve in vinegar or brine
saturate   make thoroughly wet
seethe   bubble or surge as in boiling
souse   plunge or soak in liquid

707   **stern**   adj.

severe   strict

austere   severely simple and plain
harsh   showing cruelty or lack of kindness
relentless   always without pity or let-up
rigorous   harsh and lacking in mercy
unsparing   unmerciful
unyielding   not giving way to pressure or influence

flinty   *hard-hearted*   *unbending*

708   **stirring**   adj.

exciting   rousing   stimulating

dramatic   very exciting and impressive
gripping   keeping a tight hold on a person's attention
thrilling   causing a wave of fear, excitement, or pleasure

intoxicating   *melodramatic*

709   **stomach**   n.

belly   tummy

abdomen   part of body containing stomach, bowels and digestive organs
bowels   inner, lower part of the abdomen
entrails   inside parts of an animal, especially the bowels
guts   internal organs of the abdomen
innards   stomach and bowels
intestine   tube carrying food away from the stomach
paunch   protruding belly
pot-belly   large rounded stomach

beer-belly   *bread basket*

710 stop v. (i)
cease   end   finish

abandon   give up; cease work on
desist from   not to do any more of
discontinue   put an end to; come to an
end
quit   go away from; leave; abandon
or give up a task

711 stop v. (ii)
bar   block movement or action; not to
allow
check   stop or slow the motion of
suddenly
curb   control or limit
foil   prevent from succeeding
hamper   prevent free movement or
activity
prevent   hinder; stop
prohibit   forbid by law or rule
restrain   control by holding back
suppress   put an end to the activity of;
keep from being known or seen
thwart   oppose successfully

barricade   *blockade*

712 storm n.
tempest

blizzard   long severe snowstorm
cloudburst   sudden violent rainstorm
hurricane   storm with violent wind
monsoon   seasonal heavy rains and
winds in South East Asia
tornado   violent and destructive
whirlwind advancing in a narrow
path
typhoon   violent tropical storm in the
western Pacific

duststorm   *sandstorm*   *thunderstorm*

713 story n.
account   tale

allegory   story or description in which
the characters represent good and bad
qualities
anecdote   short, amusing, or
interesting story about a real person
or event
autobiography   book written by
oneself about one's own life
biography   book of a person's life
written by someone else
chronicle   record of historical events
in the order they happened
epic   long poem, or other work of
literature, telling of heroic deeds
or history
fable   short story not based on fact,
often with animals as characters and
teaching a moral
fiction   invented story
history   record or account of past
events in the order in which they
happened
legend   story handed down from the
past which may or may not be true
memoirs   written account of events
that one has lived through
myth   traditional story containing
ideas or beliefs about ancient times
or about natural events
narration   the telling of facts, events,
or a story
novel   book-length story about
invented people
parable   story told to illustrate a
moral or spiritual truth
saga   long story with many episodes

novelette   *science fiction*

714 strange adj.
unusual

alien   foreign; very unfamiliar and
strange
curious   strange and unusual

odd   unusual and peculiar in appearance or character
outlandish   looking or sounding strange or foreign
peculiar   strange and distinct from others
quaint   odd in a pleasing way; attractive through being unusual or old-fashioned
unfamiliar   not well known; not often seen or experienced

uncommon

715   strong   adj.

powerful

brawny   strong and muscular
burly   strong and heavily built
hardy   able to bear cold, hard work, or difficult conditions
herculean   possessing very great strength
mighty   having great power or strength; very great in size
robust   healthy, strong, and vigorous
strapping   big, tall, and healthy-looking

beefy   hefty   muscle-bound

716   subject   n.

angle   point of view
gist   essential points or general sense, especially of a long statement
matter   contents of something written or spoken as distinct from its form
proposition   suggestion; something to be dealt with
text   original words of a speech, article, or book
theme   main idea or topic in a talk or piece of writing
thesis   statement or theory put forward and supported by argument
topic   subject for a speech, conversation, or written work

717   successful   adj.

booming   growing rapidly in value, importance, and prosperity
flourishing   growing and developing healthily
lucrative   bringing in plenty of money
productive   tending or able to make things, especially in large quantities
profitable   bringing money or benefits
prosperous   financially successful
thriving   doing very well

718   suddenly   adv.

abruptly   suddenly and surprisingly
hastily   said, made, or done too quickly
instantly   at once
unexpectedly   surprisingly and unforeseen

719   suggest   v.

advocate   be or speak in favour of
hint   refer indirectly to
imply   suggest without stating directly
introduce   make known or mention for the first time
propose   put forward for consideration
recommend   praise as being good for a purpose
submit   offer for consideration or decision

bring up   moot   put forward

720   sulky   adj.

morose   gloomy and unsociable
peevish   easily annoyed
petulant   showing childish temper for no reason
resentful   feeling bitter or insulted
sullen   silently showing dislike or ill temper

721 **supply** v.

provide

cater provide food and drink for
payment at a public or private party
distribute divide among several;
spread or scatter
equip supply with what is necessary
furnish supply with what is necessary
for a special purpose
provision provide with food and
supplies
replenish fill up again
satisfy give a person what he
demands or needs; fulfil or comply
with

722 **suspect** v.

distrust lack belief in; be suspicious
of
doubt be uncertain about
infer get the meaning from something
by reasoning
presume take as a fact without proof

mistrust smell a rat

723 **swear** v. (i)

depose give evidence, especially on
oath in court
pledge promise solemnly
promise declare that one will do or
not do a thing
testify bear witness to a fact; give
evidence under oath
vow promise solemnly

swear v. (ii)

curse exlaim in anger with oaths and
indecent words

724 **swollen** adj.

distended enlarged

bloated unpleasantly swollen with
fat, gas, or liquid
dilated made or become wider or
larger
dropsical swollen by watery fluid in
the tissues of the body
expanded made or become larger
inflated filled and swollen with air or
gas
puffy slightly swollen
turgid swollen by liquid or inner
pressure

over-stuffed

725 **talk** v.

address direct a remark or written
statement to
blurt out say suddenly and without
thinking
chat talk in a friendly manner
chatter talk quickly and at length
about unimportant matters
confer discuss and compare opinions
consult seek information or advice
converse exchange thoughts and
opinions; talk
declaim speak or say impressively or
dramatically
digress depart from the main subject
temporarily in speaking or writing
discuss consider by talking or writing
about
enthuse show a strong interest and
admiration through talking
gush express admiration or pleasure
in a great flow of words foolishly and
without true feeling
harangue address in an angry or
forceful way, especially to blame the
listeners
jabber talk quickly and not clearly
lecture give a talk to a group
maunder talk in a rambling, aimless
way

pontificate   speak or write as if one's judgement is the only correct one
prattle   chatter in a childish way
rage   talk or shout in a very angry way
rant   make a speech loudly, violently and showily
rave   talk wildly as if mad
spout   pour out in a stream of words
tattle   gossip about another's personal matters or secrets

flare up   fulminate   gossip   mumble mutter   preach   ramble   stammer relate

726   **tame**   adj. (i)

broken-in   made tame or disciplined by training
controllable   able to be managed
docile   obedient and easily taught or led
domesticated   animals trained to live with and be kept by man
trained   taught and accustomed to do something

tame   adj. (ii)

unexciting

727   **taste**   v.

relish   savour or enjoy to the full
savour   taste slowly and purposefully with enjoyment
try   test on one's palate to see if one likes it

728   **teach**   v.

coach   improve the skills or knowledge
cram   study for an examination by hastily memorizing
educate   train and develop the mind, abilities, and character

indoctrinate   fill a person's mind with particular ideas
instruct   give a person instruction in a subject or skill
school   discipline or control
train   give teaching or practice, especially in an art, profession, or skill
tutor   give private instruction to a single pupil or very small group

729   **teacher**   n.

coach   person who trains sportsmen and athletes, or a student for an examination
educationalist   an expert in educational methods
governess   female teacher who lives with a family and educates their children at home
guru   influential or revered teacher
instructor   one who gives information or knowledge, or teaches particular skills
lecturer   person who teaches in a college or university
mentor   trusted adviser
pedagogue   one who teaches in a dull, detailed and unimaginative way
schoolmaster   male teacher in a school
schoolmistress   female teacher in a school
trainer   person who trains athletes or animals
tutor   private teacher; university teacher directing the studies of undergraduates

730   **tease**   v.

annoy   make a little angry, especially by repeated acts
bedevil   trouble greatly
harass   trouble and annoy continually
pester   annoy with frequent requests or questions

torment   cause persistent distress to
mind or body
vex   irritate and worry

make fun of

731   **telescope**   n.

binoculars   instrument with lenses for
both eyes, making distant objects
seem nearer
field-glasses   large binoculars for
outdoor use
microscope   instrument with lens that
magnifies objects or details too small
to be seen by the naked eye
opera-glasses   small binoculars for use
at the theatre
periscope   long tube containing
mirrors so that a person lower down,
especially in a submarine, can see
what is above him
spy-glass   small telescope

732   **tell**   v.

delineate   portray in words, especially
with detail and exactness
depict   picture in words
describe   give an account of what
something is like
explain   make plain or clear; show the
meaning of
narrate   tell a story; give an account
of
portray   describe in words or
represent in a play
recount   tell in detail
relate   tell a story
report   give a factual account
sketch   describe roughly with few
details

733   **telling**   adj.

effective   revealing

cogent   compelling belief or
agreement

convincing   making a person feel
certain that something is true
forceful   strongly persuasive
suggestive   bringing new ideas to the
mind, in addition to what is expressed
weighty   showing or deserving
earnest thought

734   **temper**   n.

anger   feeling of great annoyance or
hostility
indignation   anger aroused by
something thought to be unjust or
wicked
irritability   state of being easily and
quickly annoyed by small things
peevishness   sulky fretfulness
petulance   state of unreasonable
impatience
surliness   state of bad temper and bad
manners
tantrum   outburst of bad temper,
especially in a child
wrath   great anger

hot-headedness

735   **tempt**   v.

captivate   capture the fancy of
entice   attract or persuade by offering
something pleasant
infatuate   inspire or fill with foolish,
shallow, or extravagant passion
lure   attract or tempt away from what
one should do
seduce   persuade, especially into
wrongdoing, by making it seem
attractive

736   **terrific**   adj.

*excellent   exceptional   first-class
marvellous   outstanding   sensational
smashing   splendid   spot-on
wonderful*

737 then adv.

*after that   at that time   from then on
in that case   next   subsequently
thereupon*

738 therefore adv.

*accordingly   because of
consequently   for that reason   hence
on account of   so   thus*

739 thief n.

blackmailer   person who makes
another give money by threatening to
reveal a guilty secret
burglar   person who breaks into a
building to steal
cat-burglar   thief who enters buildings
by climbing walls or drainpipes
con man   person who makes people
believe in him to cheat them
cracksman   expert in breaking into
safes
housebreaker   thief who enters houses
by force, especially during the day
mugger   person who robs another by
violence, especially in a public place
pilferer   thief who steals small things
sneak-thief   person who takes things
within reach without using force
swindler   person who cheats in a
business deal

*pick-pocket   poacher   rustler
shoplifter   smuggler*

740 thin adj.

emaciated   having become very thin
from illness or starvation
gangling   tall, thin, and awkward-
looking
gaunt   bony and emaciated in
appearance
haggard   looking exhausted and
careworn from prolonged worry,
illness, or lack of sleep
lanky   ungracefully lean and tall
lean   without much flesh
scraggy   thin and bony
scrawny   without much flesh on the
bones
skinny   very thin
slender   delicately or gracefully thin
in the body
slim   attractively and lightly built
spare   thin and lean
spindly   long, thin, and weak-looking
weedy   weakly in appearance
wiry   lean but tough and strong
wizened   dried up and wrinkled with
age

half-starved   underfed   wasted

741 thing n.

*apparatus   article   contrivance
device   gadget   instrument
machine   mechanism   object   stuff
substance   tool*

742 think v.

analyse   examine carefully in order to
find out about
brood   think long and deeply,
resentfully, or sadly
conceive   form an idea or plan in the
mind
consider   think about carefully in
order to make a decision
deliberate   think over or discuss
carefully before reaching a decision
imagine   think, believe, or guess
meditate   think deeply, seriously, and
quietly
muse   reflect about, or ponder on,
usually in silence
picture   form a mental image of
ponder   think something over
thoroughly

reason   use one's ability to think and draw conclusions

reflect   remind oneself of past events, consider

believe   concentrate on   mull over

743   through   prep. & adv.

*between   from end to end
from side to side   throughout*

744   throw   v.

cast   throw off or away
chuck   throw carelessly or casually
fling   throw violently, angrily or hurriedly
heave   lift or haul with great effort
hurl   throw with force
pitch   hurl, throw, cast, or fling
shy   throw with a quick movement
sling   throw, especially roughly or with effort
toss   throw lightly, carelessly, or easily

catapult   pitchfork

745   tie   v.

bind   tie or fasten together securely
lash   secure firmly with cord
moor   fasten a boat to a fixed object with ropes or an anchor
picket   secure or enclose with a stake or stakes
stake   fasten or strengthen with sticks or posts
strap   secure with a strip of leather or other flexible material
tether   fasten an animal with a rope or chain to limit movement
truss   tie so as to prevent all movement
yoke   harness two animals together by means of a wooden crosspiece; couple, unite

bandage   make fast

746   tight   adj.

compressed   forced into less space; squeezed tightly together
cramped   put or kept in too narrow a space, without room to move
jammed   packed tightly into a small space
taut   stretched firmly, not slack

skin-tight

747   time   n.

age   length of time a person has lived or a thing has existed
date   time shown by the number of the day, month, and year
epoch   particular period of history
era   period of time named after or starting from an important event
instant   an exact point of time; the present moment
juncture   point in time, especially a critical one
occasion   time at which a particular event takes place
season   time of year when something is common or plentiful, or when a particular activity takes place

moment   period

748   tired   adj.

bored   fed-up and not interested
exhausted   tired out and lacking all energy
fatigued   greatly tired because of much hard work or exercise
weary   very tired, especially from long effort

*all in   dead tired   dog-tired   done in
fagged out   ready to drop   spent
worn-out*

749 too adv. (i)

also   as well   in addition   moreover

too adv. (ii)

excessively

750 top n.

apex   crown   summit

acme highest point of development,
  success, or perfection
brow ridge at the top of a slope or hill
crest top of a slope, hill, mountain,
  or wave
pinnacle highest point
zenith highest point of hope,
  achievement or fortune

751 touch v.

brush touch lightly in passing
caress give a loving touch or kiss
feel explore by touch
finger feel or handle with one's
  fingers
handle touch, feel, or move with the
  hands
press apply weight or force steadily
  to a thing
stroke pass the hand over gently,
  especially to give pleasure

fondle   paw   pet

752 tough adj.

durable not wearing out or decaying
  quickly
leathery like hard skin
stubborn strong-willed and not easy
  to control or deal with
sturdy strongly-built

hard-boiled   obstinate

753 tower n.

belfry space in a tower where bells
  are hung
citadel fortress overlooking a city
cupola small dome on a roof
fortress building, place, or town
  strengthened for defence
minaret tall, slender tower forming
  part of a mosque
obelisk tall, pointed stone pillar set
  up as a monument
pagoda Indian or Far Eastern temple,
  usually shaped like a pyramid and
  having many storeys
pyramid ancient stone building with
  a flat, usually square, base and
  sloping sides that meet at the top
spire tall roof rising steeply to a point
  on top of a tower
steeple church tower rising to a high,
  sharp point
turret small tower on a building or
  defensive wall

754 trick v.

cheat

bamboozle mystify with a trick
bemuse puzzle completely
deceive make someone believe
  something which is false
defraud deceive so as to get
  something illegally
dupe deceive, especially by trickery
mislead lead astray; deceive
outmanoeuvre put in a position of
  disadvantage
outwit get the better of a person by
  one's cleverness or craftiness

hoodwink   misinform

755 truly adv.

actually   certainly   genuinely
indeed   loyally   really   sincerely
surely   truthfully   undoubtedly

756 try v.

attempt

endeavour try hard and steadily
essay make an effort to accomplish
  something
strive struggle hard to get or conquer
undertake agree or promise to do
  something; make oneself responsible
  for
venture risk going somewhere or
  doing something dangerous

757 turn v.

circle travel round, returning to the
  starting point
gyrate swing round and round a fixed
  point
pivot turn on a central point or shaft
revolve move or cause to move
  around a centre or axis
rotate turn or cause to turn round a
  fixed point
spin turn or cause to turn rapidly on
  its axis
swivel turn or swing as if on a central
  shaft
wheel move in circles or curves

758 ugly adj.

deformed badly or not normally
  shaped
disfigured with the appearance
  spoiled
grisly causing fear, horror, or disgust
gruesome shocking and sickening
ill-favoured unattractive
monstrous of unnaturally large size
  or strange shape and appearance
mutilated maimed or damaged,
  especially with an essential part cut
  off
nauseating sickening and disgusting
unsightly not pleasant to look at

repulsive

759 unconcerned adj.

aloof not joining in; distant in feeling
  or interest
distant remote in manner; unfriendly
impassive not feeling or showing
  emotion
indifferent not caring about or
  noticing
uninterested without interest
uninvolved not taking part or
  interested in the affairs of others

preoccupied *unsympathetic*
unworried

760 under prep.

below beneath underneath

761 understand v.

comprehend

apprehend grasp the meaning
discern see or understand, especially
  with difficulty
fathom get at the true meaning
grasp succeed in understanding

get the picture

762 unfair adj.

unjust

biased influenced unfairly for or
  against
one-sided seeing only one side of a
  question
prejudiced having an unreasoning
  opinion or dislike
undeserved not meriting a reward or
  punishment
unjustifiable not having a good reason
  for

unsporting

763 **unsure** adj.

uncertain

dubious doubtful
sceptical inclined to disbelieve things
unconvinced uncertain that
  something is true
undecided not yet having made up
  one's mind

doubtful suspicious unconfident

764 **up-to-date** adj.

*current fashionable fresh
in the swim latest modern
present-day recent*

765 **urgent** adj.

critical of or at a crisis
crucial of decisive importance
demanding needing a lot of attention,
  patience and skill
essential absolutely necessary
imperative extremely urgent or
  important
vital essential to the existence,
  success, or working of something

high-priority pressing serious

766 **use** v.

employ use the services of; make use
  of
exploit work or develop; use for
  one's own advantage and other
  people's disadvantage
manipulate handle, manage, or use a
  thing skilfully
manoeuvre guide a thing skilfully or
  craftily
operate control the function; cause to
  work
ply wield or use a tool or weapon;
  work at a job or trade
utilize make use of or find a use for

wield hold and use with the hands;
  have and use power

consume expend

767 **useful** adj.

effective producing the desired result
functional made for practical use
  without ornamentation
practical convenient in actual use
serviceable suitable for ordinary use
  or wear

advantageous convenient usable

768 **useless** adj.

fruitless producing little or no result
impracticable cannot be used in
  practice
ineffective not producing the desired
  result
ineffectual having no or very little
  effect
unavailing not being of any help or
  advantage

futile unprofitable unserviceable

769 **usual** adj.

customary

established widely or permanently
  accepted
habitual done regularly
routine regular and not exciting
set fixed or decided

accustomed normal

770 **value** n.

worth

usefulness

771 vehicle n.

*automobile bicycle bus car
carriage cart conveyance jeep
lorry moped motorcycle sledge
tank tractor train tram trolley
truck wagon*

772 very adv.

*deeply exceedingly exceptionally
extremely notably*

773 view n.

feature any typical or noticeable part
  of the scenery
outlook view on which one looks out
panorama view over a wide area
prospect extensive view of a
  landscape
scene landscape or view as seen by a
  spectator
setting surroundings in which
  something is placed
spectacle striking or impressive sight
vision rare or beautiful sight
vista view, especially one seen
  through a long, narrow opening, such
  as an avenue of trees

*landscape seascape scenery
skyscape*

774 vow n.

oath solemn promise; solemn
  undertaking to do something
pledge formal promise or agreement
testimony formal statement that
  something is true; information given
  on oath

*avowal promise undertaking
word-of-honour*

775 vulgar adj.

indecent offending against
  recognized standards; unseemly
lewd treating sexual matters in a low
  way
obscene indecent in a repulsive or
  very offensive way

*filthy immodest improper
shameless smutty*

776 wait v.

await wait for; be in store or ready
  for
loiter move about idly with frequent
  stops
postpone keep from happening until
  a later time
procrastinate put off action until a
  later time
tarry delay in coming or going

dally dawdle kill time

777 wakeful adj.

attentive taking careful notice
observant quick at noticing things

on guard watchful wide-awake

778 walk v.

amble walk at an easy, gentle rate
mince walk with dainty steps in an
  affected manner
pace walk with slow, regular steps
pad walk softly with the feet flat on
  the ground
plod walk with heavy, usually slow,
  steps
prowl move stealthily around as if in
  search of prey or plunder
saunter walk in an unhurried way
shamble walk or move along in an
  awkward or unsteady way

shuffle walk without lifting the feet clear of the ground

sidle move in a furtive or stealthy manner; edge along

slink move quietly and secretly, as if fearful or ashamed

stagger move or go unsteadily, as if about to fall

stride walk with long steps

stroll walk slowly for pleasure

strut walk in a pompous, self-satisfied way

swagger walk with a swinging movement, as if proud

tread step in, on, over or across

trudge walk with heavy steps, slowly and with effort

waddle walk with short steps, rocking slightly from side to side

hike   *limp*   *march*   *ramble*   *toddle*
totter   *tramp*

779 **wall** n.

barricade wall hastily built as a defence

bulkhead upright partition in a ship or aircraft

bulwark strong wall of earth built as a defence

dry-wall wall built of stones without the aid of mortar

dyke long wall or embankment to keep back water and prevent flooding

embankment long mound of earth or a stone structure to keep a river from spreading, or to carry a road or railway

paling fencing made of wooden posts or railings

rampart wide bank protecting a fort or city

screen upright structure used to conceal, protect or divide something

stockade protective fence of strong upright stakes

partition

780 **want** v.

covet desire eagerly, especially something belonging to another person

crave have a very strong longing for

desire wish or want very much

lack be without or not have a thing when it is needed

long for have an intense, persistent wish for

need want for some useful purpose

pine for become ill, feeble, or thin through longing

require need; depend on for success or fulfilment

fancy   *wish for*   *yearn for*

781 **war** n.

battle fight between enemies or opposing groups

campaign series of military operations with a set purpose, usually in one area

civil war war between groups of citizens of the same country

crusade struggle or movement against something believed to be bad

guerrilla warfare fighting or harassment by small groups acting independently against regular troops or police

hostilities acts of warfare

total war war involving civilians as well as the armed forces

warfare state of war; being engaged in war

Armageddon

782 **warm** adj.

close lacking fresh or freely-moving air

lukewarm slightly warmer than cold

mild gently agreeable weather

muggy unpleasantly damp and warm

snug warm and cosy

tepid only slightly warm

783 wash v.

clean

bath   cleanse   launder   mop
rinse   scrub   shampoo   shower
soak   sponge   swab

784 waste v.

dissipate   use up foolishly
fritter away   waste little by little,
  especially on trivial things
splurge   spend money freely and
  showily
squander   spend wastefully or
  extravagantly

deplete   exhaust   misspend

785 watch v.

gaze   look long and steadily
observe   see and notice; watch
  carefully
ogle   look at with great, especially
  sexual, interest
spy   keep watch secretly
stare   look fixedly with the eyes wide
  open
view   watch or inspect carefully
witness   be present and notice

786 wave n.

bore   very large wave caused by a tide
  running up a narrow river
breaker   heavy ocean wave that
  breaks on the coast
chop   short, broken waves
comber   long, curling wave
ground swell   heavy, slow-moving
  waves caused by a distant or recent
  storm
surf   white foam of waves breaking
  on a rock or shore
swell   heaving of the sea with waves
  that do not break

tidal wave   unusually large incoming
  wave, often caused by high winds,
  spring tides, or an earthquake

787 weak adj.

decrepit   weak or in bad condition
  from old age or hard work
delicate   liable to illness; easily
  injured; requiring careful handling
diluted   made less concentrated by
  adding water or a thinner
feeble   without strength or force
flimsy   easily broken or destroyed
fragile   easily damaged; not strong
frail   physically weak
infirm   weak in body or mind,
  especially from age or illness
puny   undersized, feeble

788 wear v.

erode   wear away gradually
fray   make clothes or material worn
  so that there are loose threads,
  especially at the edge
rub   wear by moving to and fro

789 weighty adj. (i)

heavy

bulky   very large and unwieldly;
  taking up much space
cumbersome   clumsy to wear, carry,
  or manage
hefty   large, heavy, and difficult to
  move
massive   very large and heavy, and
  usually solid
ponderous   huge and unwieldly
unwieldy   awkward to move or
  control because of its size, shape,
  or weight

790 weighty adj. (ii)

important

cogent convincing, compelling belief
momentous of very great importance
  or seriousness
persuasive having the power to
  influence others
significant of noticeable importance
  or effect
telling very effective

influential

791 wet adj.

drenched completely wet through
saturated unable to hold any more
  liquid
soaked made thoroughly wet
sodden heavy with wetness
soggy unpleasantly full of moisture
sopping completely soaked and
  dripping
waterlogged so full of water it will
  barely float; earth so wet it cannot
  be worked

792 white adj.

*chalky   creamy   ivory   marble
milky   pearly   snow-white   snowy*

793 wide adj.

all-embracing including everything
broad large across
expansive widely spread
extensive large in area
spacious having a lot of room
wide-ranging covering an extensive
  area
world-wide extending through the
  whole world

widespread

794 wind n.

cyclone very violent wind moving
  quickly in a circle round a calm centre
doldrums ocean regions near the
  equator where there is little or no
  wind
draught current or flow of air
gale very strong wind
gust sudden rush of wind
squall sudden storm of wind,
  especially with rain, snow, or sleet
trade wind belt of winds blowing
  towards the equator
zephyr soft, gentle wind

795 wise adj.

enlightened having true
  understanding
erudite having or showing great
  learning
judicious showing good sense
perceptive quick to notice and
  understand
sagacious having deep understanding
  and judgement
scholarly concerned with serious,
  detailed study; having great
  knowledge of a subject

796 wonderful adj.

*amazing   astounding   awe-inspiring
extraordinary   fantastic   magnificent
marvellous   miraculous   remarkable*

797 wood n.

afforestation process of planting with
  trees to form a forest
coppice wood of small trees and
  undergrowth, grown for periodic
  cutting
copse another word for coppice
forest large wooded area having a
  thick growth of trees and plants
grove small group of trees

plantation   area of land on which cultivated trees or plants are grown
scrub   low-growing plants including bushes and short trees growing in poor soil
spinney   small wood
thicket   number of shrubs and small trees growing close together
timber   trees for building or paper-making
woodland   wooded country

798 **work** n. (i)

labour

drudgery   hard, dull work
grind   hard, monotonous work
handiwork   work needing the skilful use of the hands
legwork   working that involves travelling on foot
odd-job   work that is not regular or fixed
spadework   hard work done in preparation for something
task   piece of work to be done
undertaking   task or enterprise; agreement to do something

799 **work** n. (ii)

employment   job   livelihood

calling   strong inner urge to follow an occupation
career   way of making a living, especially one with opportunities for advancement or promotion
craft   occupation in which skill, especially of the hands, is needed
profession   occupation requiring special training and qualifications

800 **write** v.

correspond   write letters to each other regularly

draft   make a rough, preliminary written version
draw up   decide and write down something
engrave   cut or carve into a hard surface
inscribe   write or cut words on a surface
note   keep a brief record of something
record   set down in writing or other permanent form
scrawl   write in a careless, irregular, or unskilful way
scribble   write hurriedly or carelessly
transcribe   write, type, or print out fully from speech or notes

list

801 **writing** n.

calligraphy   the art of producing beautiful handwriting
longhand   ordinary writing, contrasted with shorthand, typing, or printing
penmanship   skill in writing by hand
script   writing done by hand, especially with the letters of words joined

802 **yellow** adj.

amber   buff   butter   daffodil flaxen   gilt   gold   golden   honey jaundiced   lemon   primrose   saffron sallow   sandy   tawny

803 **young** adj.

youthful

adolescent   between being a child and an adult
childish   acting like a child; unsuitable for a grown person
immature   not fully formed or developed

infantile   acting like a small child
juvenile   of or for young people
puerile   childish; silly
teenage   between 13 and 19 years of
  age

*boyish   girlish   kittenish
puppy-like*

804   zoo   n.

aquarium   glass container for fish and
  other water animals and plants
aviary   large cage or building for
  keeping birds
bird sanctuary   an area where birds
  are protected and encouraged to
  breed
game park   enclosed area of
  grassland, usually with trees, where
  wild animals can be viewed
menagerie   collection of wild or
  strange animals in captivity, for
  exhibition
nature reserve   large enclosed area of
  land where plants and all other forms
  of wild life are protected
safari park   park in which wild
  animals are kept so that one can
  drive round in a car and look at them
vivarium   place where live animals
  are kept under natural conditions for
  study and research

Index

If the same word appears more than once in the index the headword under which it appears is also given. The headword is also given if the entry has been divided into two parts. The headwords are printed in **bold** type.

act   v.   19
act   (do)   243
action   18
active   (alive)   35
active   (busy)   133
actual   596
actually   (really)   597
actually   (truly)   755
acute   655
adage   573
adapted   319
addicted   20
addiction   361
additional, an   49
additionally   39
addle-pated   216
address   (name)   495
address   (talk)   725
adept   256
adeptness   671
adequate   (acceptable)   12
adequate   (enough)   267
adequate   (passable)   535
a different   49
a distinct   49
adjacent   (next, adj.i)   507
adjoining   (next, adj.i)   507
adjudicate   231
admirable   541
admiration   612
admire   21
admirer   295
admissible   535
admit   31
admittedly   395
admonish   644
adolescent   (boy)   121
adolescent   (girl)   342
adolescent   (young)   adj.   803
adopt   167
adore   458
adornment   232
adroit   557
adroitness   671
adulate   458
adult   22
adult   (mature)   471
advance   (boost)   117

advance   (go)   347
advance   (pay)   539
advantage   568
advantageous   767
advent   222
adversary   263
advertise   117
advise   23
advocate   (boost)   117
advocate   (suggest)   719
affable   (hearty)   373
affable   (pleasant)   550
affair   24
affair   (case)   144
affair   (event)   271
affect   v.(i)   25
affect   v.(ii)   26
affirm   (confirm)   193
affirm   (say)   640
affluent   622
afforestation   797
affray   313
affront   519
aficionado   295
afraid   27
afresh   29
after   (next, adj.ii)   507
after a fashion   592
aftermath   255
after that   737
afterwards   28
a further   49
again   29
age   747
agent   148
aggregate   44
aggressive   72
agile   30
agitate   26
agony   528
agree   v.(i)   31
agree   v.(ii)   32
agreeable   (civil)   169
agreeable   (nice)   508
agreeable   (pleasant)   550
agree to   11
aid   374
ailing   387

annual   324
annul   3
anorak   180
another   49
another time   29
anonymous   496
answer   v.(i)   50
answer   v.(ii)   51
antagonism   698
antagonist   263
antagonistic   614
anthem   687
anthology   116
anticipate   (**expect**)   279
anticipate   (**look for**, v.ii)   455
antiquated   516
anxiety   139
anyhow   adv.(i)   52
anyhow   adv.(ii)   53
anyway   52
apart from   (**besides**)   93
apart from   (**except**)   275
apartment   379
apathetic   536
apex   750
aphorism   573
apiece   250
apologize   604
appalling   307
apparatus   741
apparently   (**probably**)   566
appealing   (**charming**)   156
appealing   (**pretty**)   559
appear   v.(i)   54
appear   v.(ii)   55
appetizing   238
applaud   (**cheer**, v.i)   161
application   257
appoint   495
appointment   415
appreciate   (**know**, v.i)   427
apprehend   (**grasp**, v.ii)   352
apprehend   (**understand**)   761
apprehension   139
apprehensive   27
approach   n.   (**angle**)   45
approach   v.   56
approach   (**come**)   186
approach   (**contact**)   196

approaching   6
appropriate   adj.   319
appropriate   v.   339
appropriate, be   32
approve   31
approved   520
approximately   6
apt   319
aptitude   2
aquarium   804
aquamarine   109
Arab   381
arbitrary   589
arbitrate   231
archipelago   409
ardently   251
area   692
argue   57
argument   629
arid   108
Armageddon   781
armchair   151
aroma   643
around   58
arrangement   549
arrant   107
arrest   146
arrival   222
arrive   186
arrive at   (**reach**, v.i)   593
arrogance   561
arrogant   (**boastful**)   111
arrogant   (**proud**)   572
artful   59
artful   (**cunning**)   214
artful   (**sly**)   676
article   89
articulate   640
artless   328
as an alternative to   404
as a case in point   497
as a substitute for   404
ascend   176
as far as one can see   272
ashamed   60
ashen   357
ashen   529
asinine   666
ask   61

asphyxiate 166
aspire to 406
assail 63
assailant 263
assassinate 423
assault 63
assemble (collect) 184
assemble (make) 466
assembly 477
assent 87
assent to (accept) 11
assent to (let, v.i) 437
assert (believe) 88
assert (insist) 401
assert (say) 640
assess 62
assessment 524
assign 343
assist 374
assume (act) 19
assume (believe) 88
assumed 292
assumption 524
assurance 87
assuredly 395
as the case may be 472
astonishing 608
astounding (fabulous) 283
astounding (marvellous) 470
astounding (remarkable) 608
astounding (wonderful) 796
astraddle 17
astride 17
astute 615
as well (also) 39
as well (too, adv.i) 749
at all events 52
at all times 42
at a loss 194
at any rate 52
at ease 188
atlas 469
atoll 409
at present 514
at rest 188
at sea 194
attach 303
attaché case 75
attachment 445

attack 63
attacker 263
attain (reach, v.i) 593
attainable 555
attar 643
attempt 756
attentive (alert) 34
attentive (wakeful) 777
at that time 737
at the top 7
at times 685
attitude (angle) 45
attitude 64
attitude (opinion) 524
attract 65
attract (lure) 461
attraction 445
attractive (charming) 156
attractive (lovely) 459
attractive (nice) 508
attractive (pretty) 559
attribute 155
atrocious 307
auburn 66
audacity 160
audience 211
augment 393
auspicious 163
austere 707
authentic 596
authenticate 664
authorize (allow) 37
authorize (let) 437
authorized 520
authoritative 520
autobiography 713
automatic 360
automobile (car) 138
automobile (vehicle) 771
available 595
avant-garde 486
avaricious (greedy, adj.i) 356
avenue 624
average 67
aviary 804
avidly 251
avoid 245
avowal 774
await (wait) 776

bleached   529
bleak   108
blight   400
blind   223
blinding   (**brilliant**)   127
blinding   (**dazzling**)   224
blitz   63
blizzard   712
bloated   724
block   166
blockade   (**close**)   177
blockade   (**stop**, v.ii)   711
bloodless   529
bloodshot   601
bloodthirsty   212
bloom   324
blossom   324
blubber   213
bludgeon   377
blue   adj.(i)   109
blue   adj.(ii)   110
blue   (**sad**)   632
Blue Peter   320
bluff   376
blunder   485
blunderbuss   360
blunt   328
blurt out   725
blustering   111
board   309
boastful   111
boat   112
boater   368
boatload   450
body   211
bog   113
boggy   491
bogus   292
bold   114
bolt   (**bar**)   78
bolt   (**eat**)   253
bolt together   416
bombard   63
bona fide   596
bond   303
bonnet   368
bonus   115
boob   485
book   116

booming   717
boorish   631
boost   117
booty   565
border   (**boundary**)   119
border   (**edge**)   254
bordering   (**next**, adj.i)   507
border on   (**reach**, v.ii)   593
bore   786
bored   748
boring   118
boring   (**dull**)   249
bossy   521
botch   132
botched   490
bother   335
bothersome   48
bottle   197
boulevard   624
bounce   419
bouncy   (**hearty**)   373
bouncy   (**jaunty**)   413
bound   419
boundary   119
boundary   (**edge**)   254
bounds   119
bountiful   489
bouquet   (**flower**)   324
bouquet   (**scent**)   643
bout   313
boutique   660
bowed down   142
bowels   709
bowie knife   426
bowl   197
bowler   368
box   120
box   (**container**)   197
box   (**seat**)   648
boy   121
boycott   79
boyish   803
brace   602
brackish   634
bragging   111
brain-power   481
brainy   175
braise   202
branch   170

by the way   392

cabinet   120
cable   626
cackle   434
caddy   120
cadence   621
cagey   676
cajole   181
calamitous   306
calamity   13
calculating   59
call   495
calligraphy   801
calling   799
callous   130
call out   663
calm   adj.(i)   136
calm   adj.(ii)   137
camouflage   375
campaign   781
candid   328
cannon   360
canny   59
canoe   112
cap   368
capability   2
capable   256
capaciousness   692
capacity   (**ability**)   2
capacity   (**space**)   692
cape   429
capricious   518
captivate   735
captivating   (**charming**)   156
captivating   (**pretty**)   559
captive   562
capture   v.   146
car   138
car   (**vehicle**)   771
carbine   360
carbon   203
cardinal   601
care   139
career   799
care for   458
careful   140
careful, be   95

careless   141
careless   (**remiss**)   610
carelessly   53
caress   751
careworn   142
cargo   450
carmine   601
carouse   246
carp   493
carpet bag   75
carriage   771
carrier   75
carry   143
cart   v.   143
cart   n.   771
carton   120
carve   215
cascade   v.   323
cascade   n.   623
case   144
casket   120
cast   744
cast around for   454
cast aspersions on   104
castigate   644
cast-offs   420
casual   adj.(i)&(ii)   145
casual   (**random**)   589
casually   392
catalogue   n.   446
catalogue   v.   512
catapult   744
cataract   623
catastrophe   13
catastrophic   306
cat-burglar   739
catcall   663
catch   146
catching   147
catchphrase   673
category   170
cater   721
catnap   672
cause   v.   128
cause   n.   148
caustic   102
cautious   140
cavalcade   567
cavil   57

cease 710
celebrate 149
celebrated 150
celebrity 293
cement 303
censure 192
cerise 601
certainly (absolutely) 8
certainly (truly) 755
certainty 87
certificate 530
certified 520
chafe 630
chagrined 60
chain v. 416
chain n. 488
chair 151
chair (seat) 648
chalice 346
chalky 792
challenge 236
champion 295
chance (accidental) 14
chance (happen) 364
chance (random) 589
chance upon (find) 314
chance upon (meet) 476
change v. (affect, v.i) 25
change v. 152
changeable 153
change into 81
chant v. 667
chant n. 687
chaos 154
chaotic 480
character 155
character (nature) 500
characterize 235
characteristic 397
charge 560
charitable 508
charm 65
charming 156
charming (lovely) 459
chart 469
charter v. 438
charter n. 530
chary 140
chase 157

chaste 575
chastise 644
chat 725
chattels 350
chatter (shake) 656
chatter (talk) 725
cheap 158
cheat 159
check 711
cheek 160
cheer 161
cheerful (bright, adj.ii) 126
cheerful 162
cheerfully 345
cheering 163
cheering (nice) 508
cheerless (bleak) 108
cheerless 164
cheery 162
cheese-paring 483
chequered 153
cherish 458
cherry 601
chest 120
chestnut 417
chew 253
chide (rebuke) 599
chide (scold) 644
chief 464
chiefly 165
chiefly (mainly) 465
child (boy) 121
child (girl) 342
childish (silly) 666
childish (young) 803
chilly 183
chime 690
china 210
chip 123
chirp 667
chivalrous 122
chock-a-block 332
choke 166
choose 167
chop 786
chore 415
chortle 434
christen 495
chronic 168

convertible 138
convey (carry) 143
convey (say) 640
conveyance 771
convince 543
convincing 733
convict v. 192
convict n. 562
conviction 524
cook 202
cool 137
cool-headed 137
cooperate 374
copper 66
coppice 797
copse 797
copy 203
copy (likeness) 444
coracle 112
cordage 626
cordial 373
corpulent 304
correct 204
correct (proper) 571
correct v. 620
correlate 189
correspond (agree, v.ii) 32
correspond (write) 800
corresponding 635
corroborate 193
corroboration 570
corrupt adj. (bad) 74
corrupt adj. 205
corrupt v. (infect) 400
cortège 567
cost 560
costly 227
cosy 188
cot 82
cottage 379
couch 648
counsel 23
countenance 284
counterfeit n. 203
counterfeit adj. 291
count on 279
country 429
coupé 138
courageous 122

courteous 169
cove 80
covert 704
covet 780
covetous 414
cowardly 27
cower 208
crack 123
crack-brained 216
crack-of-dawn 221
cracksman 739
cradle 82
craft (boat) 112
craft (work, n.ii) 799
crafty (artful) 59
crafty (cunning) 214
crafty (sly) 676
craggy 411
cram 728
crammed 332
cramped 746
crash v. 123
crash n. 206
crate 120
crave 780
craven 27
crave for 458
crawl 207
craze (fashion, n.i) 301
craziness 511
crazy 216
creak 690
creamy 792
create (found) 327
create (invent) 408
creative 615
creator 148
creature 47
credible 555
creek 80
creep 207
creep up 176
crest (feather) 308
crest (top) 750
crestfallen 632
crib 82
criminal 74
crimson 601
cringe 208

crisis   552
crisp   209
criterion   182
critical   (**serious**)   655
critical   (**urgent**)   765
criticize   619
crockery   210
croft   300
crony   330
croon   667
crop   309
crop up   364
cross   (**angry**)   46
cross   (**mad**)   462
cross-question   273
crosswise   17
crouch   668
crowd   211
crowing   111
crowned head   425
crucial   765
crude   (**awkward**)   72
crude   (**sketchy**)   670
cruel   212
cruel   (**savage**)   637
cruise   418
crumbly   682
crusade   781
crush   (**break**)   123
crush   (**defeat**)   233
crush   (**quell**)   581
cry   213
cry   (**shout**)   663
cry out   663
crystallized   683
cuff   377
cull   167
cumbersome   (**awkward**, adj.i)   71
cumbersome   (**weighty**, adj.i)   789
cunning   (**artful**)   59
cunning   214
cunning   (**sly**)   676
cupola   753
curb   711
curdled   691
curious   714
curls   362
current   764
curse   (**swear**, v.ii)   723

cursory   584
curt   631
curtly   (**shortly**, adv.ii)   662
curve   90
cushion   648
custom   (**habit**)   361
custom   (**manner**)   467
custom   (**practice**)   556
customary   (**regular**)   605
customary   (**usual**)   769
cut   215
cutlass   426
cyclone   794

daffodil   802
daft   216
dagger   426
daily   506
dainty   559
dally   776
damage   699
damp   217
damp down   582
danger   218
dangerous   74
dangle   363
dank   217
daring   114
dark   219
dart aside   245
data   428
date   747
dated   220
daub   185
dauntless   122
Davy Jones's locker   647
dawdle   776
dawdling   674
dawn   n.(i)   221
dawn   n.(ii)   222
daybreak   221
daze   223
dazzle   223
dazzle   (**shine**)   658
dazzling   (**brilliant**)   127
dazzling   224
dead   adj.(i)   225
dead   adj.(ii)   226

deplete   784
depose   (**swear**, v.i)   723
deposit   577
depraved   205
depressed   (**blue**, adj.ii)   110
depressed   (**sad**)   632
depressing   164
deride   236
derisive   636
descant   687
describe   732
description   546
descry   649
desert   1
deserted   452
deserve   240
design   408
desirable   349
desire   v.   (**love**)   458
desire   v.   (**want**)   780
desist from   710
desolate   108
despicable   (**nasty**, adj.ii)   499
despicable   (**rotten**, adj.i)   628
despise   369
despondent   (**blue**, adj.ii)   110
despondent   (**sad**)   632
destitute   554
destroy   241
desultory   589
detached   (**fair**)   289
detached   (**loose**)   456
detail   285
detain   237
detention centre   412
determine   231
detest   369
detestable   (**rotten**, adj.i)   628
detrimental   306
devastate   241
develop   243
develop into   81
device   741
devise   (**invent**)   408
devise   (**make**)   466
devoted   290
devoted to   20
devotee   295
devour   253

devout   348
dexterity   671
dextrous   557
diabolical   637
diary   116
dictate   525
dictionary   116
differentiate   189
diffident   665
dig   410
digress   725
dilatory   610
dilated   724
dilemma   552
diligence   538
diluted   787
dim   v.   286
dim   adj.   287
dimensions   669
diminutive   (**little**)   447
diminutive   (**small**)   677
din   509
dine   253
dinghy   112
dingy   164
dip into   594
diploma   530
directive   525
directory   446
dirk   426
disagreement   580
disappear   286
disapprove   515
disarranged   490
disaster   13
disastrous   306
disburse   (**pay**)   539
disburse   (**spend**)   697
discard   1
discern   (**see**)   649
discern   (**understand**)   761
discharge   243
disclaim   239
disclose   618
discomfort   528
disconcert   223
discontinue   710
discontinued   516
discord   580

doubt   v.   722
doubtful   763
doubtless   566
doughy   682
dove-grey   357
down   (**feather**)   308
down   (**hair**)   362
down-and-out   554
down-at-heel   650
downcast   110
down-hearted   632
down-in-the-dumps   632
downpour   588
downs   354
dowry   340
doze   672
drab   164
draft   800
drag   574
dramatic   708
dramatize   259
draught   794
draw   574
draw near   56
draw up   466
dreaded   69
dreadful   (**awful**)   69
dreadful   (**fearful**)   307
dreary   (**cheerless**)   164
dreary   (**dark**)   219
dregs   (**junk**)   420
dregs   (**rabble**)   587
drenched   791
dress down   599
drifting   325
drink   246
drive   (**energy**)   264
drive   (**road**)   624
drivel   511
drizzle   588
drizzly   217
droop   247
droop   (**hang**)   363
drop   577
dropsical   724
drowse   672
drudgery   798
dry as dust   249
dry-wall   779

dubious   763
duck   245
due   248
duel   313
duffle bag   75
duffle coat   180
dugout   112
dull   249
dull   (**slow**)   675
dull-witted   675
dumbfound   223
dumbfounded   695
dumbstruck   695
dune   376
dupe   754
duplicate   n.   203
duplicate   adj.   635
duplicity   229
durable   752
during   390
dustbin   197
duststorm   712
duty   560
dwarfed   677
dwarfish   447
dwelling   379
dye   185
dynamic   35
dynamo   265

each   250
eager   413
eagerly   251
earlier   (**before**)   84
earlier   (**former**)   326
earliest   318
early light   221
earn   339
earnest   655
earthenware   210
easily   252
easy-going   435
easy chair   151
eat   253
eavesdropper   134
ebb   617
ebony   103
eccentric   518

enquiry 583
enraged (**angry**) 46
enraged (**mad**) 462
enshroud 375
ensign 320
ensnare 461
ensuing (**next**, adj.ii) 507
enter 512
enterprise 18
entertaining (**enjoyable**) 266
entertaining (**interesting**) 407
entertainment 333
enthuse 725
enthusiast 295
enthusiastic 449
enthusiastically 251
entice (**lure**) 461
entice (**tempt**) 735
enticing 156
entire (**all**) 36
entirely (**altogether**) 41
entirely (**quite**, adv.i) 586
entitle 495
entitled to, be 240
entrails 709
entrancing 156
entreat 181
enunciate 640
envious 414
envy v. 86
envy n. 698
epic 713
epigram 573
episode 24
epoch 747
equable 270
equip 721
equipment 89
equipped 595
equitable 289
era 747
eradicate 3
erect (**build**) 131
erect (**make**) 466
ere long 688
erode 788
erratic 396
error 485
ersatz (**false**) 292

erstwhile 684
erudite 795
erudition 428
escape 268
escarpment 488
escort (**bring**) 128
escort (**guard**) 358
especially 165
espy 649
essay v. 756
essence 643
essential 269
essential 765
essentially 165
establish (**begin**) 85
establish (**found**) 327
established 769
esteem 21
esteemed 294
estimate v. 359
estimate n. 560
estimation 612
estranged 451
estuary 80
eternal 228
eternally 42
evade (**escape**) 268
evaluate 62
even 270
even-handed 289
even if 40
even so 382
event 271
event (**happening**) 365
even-tempered 137
even though (**although**) 40
even though (**if**) 385
everyday (**ordinary**) 527
everlasting 228
everlastingly 42
evermore 42
every time 42
evidence 570
evident 517
evidently 272
evil 74
evolve into 81
examine (**compare**) 189
examine 273

example   274
exceedingly   772
excellent   (perfect)   541
excellent   (terrific)   736
except   (but)   135
except   275
exceptional   736
exceptionally   772
excess   276
excessively   (too, adv.ii)   749
exchange   277
exciting   278
exciting   (stirring)   708
exclaim   337
exclude   79
excluding   275
excursion   418
execrate   369
execute   (do)   243
execute   (kill)   423
exemplar   274
exemplary   541
exertion   257
exhale   124
exhaust   784
exhausted   (bleak)   108
exhausted   (careworn)   142
exhausted   (faint, adj.ii)   288
exhausted   (tired)   748
exhibit   (show)   664
exhilarate   402
exhilaration   551
exile   77
expand   393
expanded   724
expanse   692
expansive   793
expect   279
expect   (look for, v.ii)   455
expected   248
expediently   569
expedite   374
expedition   418
expeditious   403
expel   77
expend   (spend)   697
expend   (use)   766
expense   560
expensive   227

experienced   280
experienced   (practised)   557
experimental   486
expert   (efficient)   256
expert   (practised)   557
expertise   671
expiration   261
explain   281
explain   (tell)   732
explain exactly   235
explanation   148
explicit   517
exploit   (abuse, v.i)   9
exploit   n.   (act)   18
exploit   v.   (use)   766
explore   282
expostulate   515
expound   281
express   640
expression   284
expressionless   106
exquisite   559
extend   (increase)   393
extend   (reach, v.ii)   593
extensive   793
extinct   225
extinguish   582
extol   149
extra, an   49
extraordinary   (fabulous)   283
extraordinary   (marvellous)   470
extraordinary   (special)   693
extraordinary   (wonderful)   796
extremely   772
extremity   (edge)   254
extremity   (plight)   552
extricate   638
exuberant   (rank, adj.i)   590
eye   v.   702
eye-witness   694

fable   713
fabulous   283
fabulous   (fantastic, adj.ii)   297
face   284
face   (reputation)   612
face up to   476
facilitate   (boost)   117

gifted   175
gigantic   97
giggle   434
gilt   802
girl   342
girlish   803
gist   716
give   343
give away   94
give permission   37
give the slip   245
glacial   183
glad   344
gladden   (**cheer**, v.ii)   161
gladly   345
glamorous   459
glance   453
glance over   594
glare   (**shine**)   658
glare   (**stare**)   702
glaring   107
glass   346
glassy   680
gleam   658
glean   184
glee   551
glide   323
gliding   325
glimmer   658
glimpse   453
glint   658
glisten   658
glitter   658
globe-trotting   418
gloomy   (**cheerless**)   164
gloomy   (**dark**)   219
glorious   463
glossy   (**bright**)   125
glossy   (**smooth**)   680
glow   658
glower   331
glowing   125
glue   303
glum   110
glut   v.   253
glut   n.   276
glutted   332
gluttonous   (**greedy**, adj.ii)   356
go   347

goal   (**aim**)   33
goal   (**end**, n.ii)   262
go back   617
gobble up   253
gobbledegook   511
goblet   346
god-forsaken   298
godparents   531
goggle   702
gold   802
golden   802
golden-brown   66
good-looking   459
gorge   253
gorged   332
gorgeous   (**magnificent**)   463
gorgeous   (**pretty**)   559
gossip   n.   134
gossip   v.   725
gouge   171
governess   729
governmental   520
go without   239
grab   146
graceful   559
grand   463
grange   300
grant   (**agree**, v.i)   31
grant   (**allow**)   37
granting   385
granting that   40
graph   469
grapple   351
grasp   v.(i)   351
grasp   v.(ii)   352
grasp   (**know**, v.i)   427
grasp   (**understand**)   761
grasping   (**greedy**, adj.i)   356
grass   353
grassland   354
grate   v.   630
grate   n.   690
gratification   551
gratified   344
gratifying   550
gratuity   340
grave   355
graze   (**feed**)   309
graze   (**scratch**)   645

great 463
great deal, a 489
greatcoat 180
greedy adj.(i) & (ii) 356
green 353
green-eyed 414
grey 357
grid 469
grief 139
grieve 604
grievous 101
grim 355
grimace (**frown**) 331
grimace (**smile**) 679
grimy 103
grin 679
grind v. (**break**) 123
grind n. (**effort**) 257
grind n. (**work**, n.i) 798
grip n. 75
grip v. 351
gripping 708
grisly 758
groan 690
groove 361
gross 304
grotesque (**odd**) 518
ground 429
ground swell 786
group (**class**) 170
group (**crowd**) 211
grouping 526
grove 797
grovel 208
grow dull 286
grow into 81
grown-up 22
grudging 474
gruesome 758
gruffly (**shortly**, adv.ii) 662
grumble 493
guard 358
guard against 95
guarded 633
guardian 531
guerrilla warfare 781
guess 359
guffaw 434
guide 23

guideline 182
guileful 214
guileless 328
gulf 80
gulp (**drink**) 246
gulp (**gasp**) 337
gulp down 253
gun 360
gunmetal-grey 357
guru 729
gush (**flow**) 323
gush (**talk**) 725
gust 794
gut 241
guts 709
guy 626
guzzle 246
gyrate 757

habit 361
habit (**practice**) 556
habitable 448
habitation 379
habitual (**regular**) 605
habitual (**usual**) 769
habitually 522
hacienda 300
haggard (**careworn**) 142
haggard (**thin**) 740
hair 362
half-baked 216
half-starved 740
halyard 626
hammock 82
hamper n. 197
hamper v. 711
handbag 75
handbook 116
handiness 671
handiwork 798
handle 751
handout 115
handsome 559
handy 201
hang 363
hang (**kill**) 423
hanging 325
haphazard (**accidental**) 14

hinder (**delay**) 237
hindmost 431
hint (**say**) 640
hint (**suggest**) 719
hire 560
hire out 438
historic 228
history 713
hit 377
hitch 303
hit upon 314
hoard n. 371
hoard v. 639
hoax 229
hoi polloi 587
hoist 441
hold 351
holdall 75
hold dear 458
hold on to 422
hold responsible 104
holiday 378
holler 663
holocaust 317
home 379
homeland 429
homelike 188
homely 380
homeopath 244
homestead 300
honey 802
honour 21
honourable 348
hoodwink 754
hooked 20
hop 419
hopper 197
horde 211
horizontal 321
horror 642
horse 381
host 211
hostile 614
hostilities 781
hotch-potch 179
hot-headed 591
hot-headedness 734
house 379
houseboat 112

housebreaker 739
housing estate 379
hovering 325
however 382
however (**nevertheless**) 505
howl 690
howitzer 360
hubbub 509
huddle 179
huge 97
hullabaloo 509
hum 667
human beings 540
humankind 540
humble (**meek**) 475
humble (**modest**) 487
humdrum 118
humid 217
humiliate 519
humiliated 60
humiliating 657
hummock 376
humorous 334
hunk 532
hunker down 668
hunt 157
hunt for 454
hurl 744
hurricane 712
hurriedly 367
hurt v. (**affect**, v.ii) 26
hurt v. 383
husband 639
hushed 585
hymn v. 667

icy (**cold**) 183
icy (**smooth**) 680
idea 384
ideal 541
identical 635
identify 495
idle 435
idiosyncrasy 155
idiosyncratic 518
idiotic 666
idolize 458
if 385

ignoble   657
ignominious   657
ignore   386
ill   387
ill-adapted   71
ill-favoured   758
ill-natured   499
illusory   (**fantastic**)   296
illusory   (**imaginary**)   388
illustration   274
illustrious   294
ill will   698
imaginable   443
imaginary   388
imagine   (**picture**)   545
imagine   (**think**)   742
imbibe   246
imitation   203
imitating   291
immaculate   575
immaterial   553
immature   803
immediate   403
immediately   (**now**)   514
immediately   (**promptly**)   569
immense   97
immensity   692
immerse   706
immodest   775
immoral   (**bad**)   74
immoral   (**corrupt**)   205
immortal   (**deathless**)   228
immortal   (**lasting**)   430
immune   633
impair   699
impart   618
impartial   (**fair**)   289
impartial   (**just**)   421
impassive   759
impecunious   554
impede   237
impel   576
impenetrable   683
imperative   765
imperceptible   391
imperishable   (**deathless**)   228
imperishable   (**lasting**)   430
impermeable   683
impertinent   631

imperturbable   137
impetuous   591
impish   501
implacable   212
imply   719
impolite   631
important   (**serious**)   655
important   (**weighty**, adj.ii)   790
impose on   9
imposing   608
impoverished   554
impracticable   768
impregnable   633
impress   402
impression   (**feeling**)   310
impression   (**idea**)   384
impression   (**opinion**)   524
impressive   608
impress upon   25
improbable   299
improper   (**naughty**, adj.ii)   502
improper   (**shameful**)   657
improper   (**vulgar**)   775
improve   v.(i) & (ii)   389
improvident   610
impudence   160
impudent   631
impute   15
in   390
inaccessible   298
inaccuracy   485
inactive   536
in addition   (**besides**)   93
in addition   (**too**, adv.i)   749
in addition   (**also**)   39
in all directions   58
in all likelihood   566
in all parts   58
inane   666
inanimate   225
in any case   (**anyhow**, adv.i)   52
in any case   (**nevertheless**)   505
inappropriate   71
inarticulate   695
in a stupor   194
inattentive   141
inaudible   391
incandescent   125
in case   436

knead   630
knell   690
knife   426
knock   377
knock back   246
knock off   (**kill**)   423
knock off   (**rob**)   625
knoll   376
know   v.(i) & (ii)   427
know-how   671
knowing   59
knowledge   428
knowledgeable   557

labour   798
lacerate   171
lack   780
lad   121
lag   237
lager   83
lagging   674
laid up   387
lament   604
lamentable   537
land   429
landscape   773
languish   247
lanky   740
lapis lazuli   109
large   97
large quantity   457
lash   745
lass   342
lassie   342
lasting   430
lastly   431
late   (**former**)   326
late   432
late   (**sometime**)   684
lately   433
later   28
latest   764
laugh   434
laughable   666
launch   v.   85
launch   n.   112
launder   783
laundered   172

lavish   622
law   182
lawful   520
lawn   353
lax   398
lay   577
lay down   235
lay out   697
laze   (**lie**, v.i)   440
lazy   435
lead   128
leaden   357
leading question   583
leak   618
lean   740
leap   419
leapfrog   419
learning   428
lease   438
leathery   752
leave   1
leave-taking   534
leavings   420
lecture   (**rebuke**)   599
lecture   (**talk**)   725
lecturer   729
ledger   116
leer   453
leeway   692
left-overs   420
legal   520
legend   713
legitimate   520
legwork   798
leisurely   674
lemon   802
lend   438
lend a hand   374
lenient   398
lest   436
let   (**allow**)   37
let   v.(i)   437
let   v.(ii)   438
lethal   305
lethargic   435
level   (**even**)   270
level   (**flat**)   321
lever   441
levy   560

lewd   775
liable to   595
liar   439
libeller   439
liberate   613
licence   530
licensed   520
lie   v.(i) & (ii)   440
lifeless   225
lift   441
light-footed   30
light-hearted   162
light upon   314
light-weight   447
like   442
likeable   508
likely   443
likely   566
liken   189
likeness   (**copy**)   203
likeness   444
liking   445
lilt   621
limit   (**boundary**)   119
limit   (**edge**)   254
limp   adj.   682
limp   v.   778
limousine   138
limpid   173
lineaments   284
liner   659
line-up   446
linger   237
link   416
liquidate   423
list   n.   446
list   v.   800
literal   204
litter   179
little   447
little   (**small**)   677
liveable   448
livelihood   (**job**)   415
livelihood   (**work**, n.ii)   799
lively   (**bright**)   126
lively   449
load   (**heap**)   371
load   450
load   (**lot**)   457

loaded question   583
loathe   v.   369
loathing   198
loathsome   (**rotten**, adj.i)   628
locale   603
locate   (**find**)   314
locate   (**put**)   577
lock   78
locker   120
lock up   v.   78
lock-up   n.   412
lodge   703
lodgings   379
log   116
logical   598
loiter   776
loll   (**lie**, v.i)   440
lonely   adj.(i)   451
lonely   adj.(ii)   452
long for   780
longhand   801
long-lived   430
long-standing   168
look   453
look as if   55
look black   331
look daggers   331
look for   v.(i)   454
look for   v.(ii)   455
look for   (**seek**)   651
look like   55
look up   196
look up to   21
loom   54
loop   90
loose   (**baggy**)   76
loose   456
loot   565
lorry   771
lorryload   450
lot   (**amount**)   44
lot   457
lottery   564
lounge   668
loutish   631
love   458
lovely   459
lovely   (**pretty**)   559
lowly   475

massive 789
masterful 557
masterly 256
mastery 2
masticate 253
match v. 32
match n. 336
matching 635
matter (case) 144
matter (subject) 716
mature (adult) 22
mature 471
mature (ready) 595
mature into 81
maunder 725
maxim 573
maybe 472
maybe (perhaps) 542
meadow 353
meagre 311
mean adj.(i) 473
mean adj.(ii) 474
meander 90
meandering 396
meaningless 553
mean spirited 474
measure 189
measurements 669
mechanism 741
meddler 134
meddlesome 521
meditate 742
meditative 655
meek 475
meet 476
meeting 477
melodramatic 708
melody 687
menagerie 804
memoirs 713
memorable 693
memorize 609
menace 218
menacing 655
mend 478
mendacious 292
mentality 481
mental state 64
mention 495

mentor 729
mercenary (greedy, adj.i) 356
merchandise (goods) 350
merchandise (load) 450
merchantman 659
merciless 130
merely 479
merit 240
merriment 333
merry 162
mess 179
messy 480
method (manner) 467
methodical 606
meticulous 140
microscope 731
middling (average) 67
middling (passable) 535
midget 447
mighty 715
mild (beer) 83
mild (gentle) 338
mild (warm) 782
milky 792
minaret 753
mince 778
mind 481
mind-boggling 278
mindful 68
mindlessly 53
miniature 677
minor (boy) 121
minor (girl) 342
minor (petty) 544
minority 532
minute 677
minx 342
miraculous (fabulous) 283
miraculous (marvellous) 470
miraculous (wonderful) 796
mire 113
mirth 333
miry 491
misadventure 13
misapply 9
misappropriate 625
miscalculation 485
mischance 13
miser 482

miserable   632
miserly   (**mean**, adj.ii)   474
miserly   483
misfortune   13
migiving   (**qualm**)   579
misgiving   (**care**)   139
mishap   365
misinform   754
mislead   754
mismanage   132
miss   n.   342
miss   v.   604
misspend   784
mist   484
mistake   485
mistrust   722
misty   217
misunderstanding   485
misuse   9
mitre   v.   303
mitre   n.   368
mixed up   194
moan   690
mob   (**crowd**)   211
mob   (**rabble**)   587
mode   (**fashion**, n.i)   301
mode   (**manner**)   467
moderate   67
modern   486
modern   (**up-to-date**)   764
modest   487
modify   (**affect**, v.i)   25
modify   (**change**)   152
moist   217
moment   747
momentous   790
monarch   425
moneyed   622
money-grubbing   483
monotonous   (**boring**)   118
monotonous   (**dull**)   249
monsoon   712
monstrous   758
moor   n.   354
moor   v.   745
moot   719
mop   783
moped   771
moral   348

morals   182
morass   113
more exactly   592
more or less   (**about**)   6
more or less   (**nearly**)   503
moreoever   (**too**, adv.i)   749
more truly   592
morose   (**sulky**)   720
morsel   99
mortal   305
mortals   540
mortar   360
mostly   465
mother   531
mother country   429
motive   148
motor   265
motorcade   567
motorcar   138
motorcycle   771
motorway   624
motto   673
moulder   627
mouldy   (**rotten**, adj.ii)   628
mouldy   (**stale**)   701
mound   376
mount   176
mountain   488
mourn   213
mouth   n.   80
mouth   v.   640
mouthful   99
move   26
move closer to   56
move steathily   207
move towards   186
much   489
muckraker   134
mucky   491
muddled   (**confused**)   194
muddled   490
muddy   491
mugger   739
muggy   (**damp**)   217
muggy   (**warm**)   782
mull over   742
multitude   211
multitudinous   468
mumble   725

munch 253
murder 423
murderous 312
murky 164
muscle-bound 715
muse 742
musket 360
must 492
mustang 381
muster 184
musty 701
muted (**inaudible**) 391
muted (**quiet**) 585
mutilated 758
mutter 725
mystery 578
mystified (**confused**) 194
myth 713

nab 351
nag n. 381
nag v. 493
nagging 48
naked 494
name 495
name (**reputation**) 612
nameless 496
namely 497
nap 672
narrate 732
narration 713
narrow-minded 474
nasty (**awful**, adj.ii) 70
nasty adj.(i) 498
nasty adj.(ii) 499
nation 540
native land 429
naturally 329
nature (**character**) 155
nature 500
nature reserve 804
naughty (adj.i) 501
naughty (adj.ii) 502
nauseating (**smelly**) 678
nauseating (**ugly**) 758
nearby 201
nearly (**almost**) 38
nearly 503

near to 91
necessary 269
need 780
needy 554
neglect (**ignore**) 386
neglect 504
neglectful (**careless**) 141
neglectful (**remiss**) 610
negligent (**careless**) 141
negligent (**remiss**) 610
negligently 53
never-ending 430
nervous 27
net 146
nettled (**angry**) 46
nettled (**mad**) 462
neutral 421
nevertheless (**but**) 135
nevertheless (**however**) 382
nevertheless 505
newborn 73
newsmonger 134
newspaper 506
newsprint 530
next adj.(i) & (ii) 507
next (**then**) 737
next to 91
nibble 253
nice 508
nick 625
nick-nack 232
niggardly 483
nimble 30
noble (**good**, adj.i) 348
noble (**magnificent**) 463
nod off 672
noise 509
noisome 678
nominate 495
nonchalant (**casual**, adj.i) 145
none 510
none the less 505
non-participating 536
nonplus 223
non-plussed 194
non-plussed 695
nonsense 511
nonsensical 666
no-one 510

no part   510
normal   (**average**)   67
normal   (**regular**)   605
normal   (**usual**)   769
nosegay   324
nose out   651
not a bit   510
notably   772
not all there   216
not any   510
notched   411
not counting   275
note   512
note   (**write**)   800
noteworthy   693
not here   258
nothing more than   479
notice   649
notify   196
notion   (**idea**)   384
not long ago   433
not many   311
not often   652
not one   510
notoriety   293
notorious   513
not present   258
not quite   (**almost**)   38
not quite   (**nearly**)   503
not quite   (**scarcely**)   641
not relevant to   91
not withstanding   505
nourish   309
novel   (**book**)   116
novel   adj.   486
novel   (**story**)   713
novelette   713
now   514
now and again   685
nude   494
nudge   576
number   44
nullify   3
numerous   468
nursling   73
nurture   309

oath   774

obelisk   753
obese   304
object   n.   (**aim**)   33
object   n.   (**end**)   262
object   v.   515
object   n.   (**thing**)   741
objectionable   498
objective   n.   262
objective   adj.   421
obliged to, be   492
obliging   (**decent**)   230
obnoxious   498
obscene   775
obscure   (**faint, adj.i**)   287
obscure   (**nameless**)   496
observance   556
observant   (**aware**)   68
observant   (**wakeful**)   777
observation   524
observe   (**celebrate**)   149
observe   (**watch**)   785
observer   694
obsolescent   220
obsolete   (**dated**)   220
obsolete   516
obstinate   752
obtain   339
obstruct   166
obtrusive   107
obtuse   675
obvious   517
obviously   272
occasion   (**event**)   271
occasion   (**time**)   747
occasionally   685
occupation   415
occupiable   448
occupied   133
occur   364
occurrence   (**event**)   271
occurrence   (**happening**)   365
ocean   647
odd   518
odd   (**strange**)   714
odd-job   798
odds and ends   420
odious   242
odour   643
offend   519

peculate   625
peculiar   (**odd**)   518
peculiar   (**strange**)   714
pedagogue   729
peep   453
peer   453
peeved   (**angry**)   46
peeved   (**mad**)   462
peevish   720
peevishness   734
pelt   362
penal institution   412
penalty   560
penchant   445
peninsula   429
penitentiary   412
penmanship   801
pennant   320
penniless   554
penny-pinching   483
penthouse   379
penurious   554
people   540
per   250
perceive   649
perceptive   795
perch   668
perennial   324
perfect   541
perform   243
performance   18
perfume   643
perfunctory   610
perhaps   (**maybe**)   472
perhaps   542
peril   218
perimeter   (**boundary**)   119
perimeter   (**edge**)   254
period   747
periodically   522
periphery   (**boundary**)   119
periphery   (**edge**)   254
periscope   731
perish   627
perished   225
perjurer   439
permanent   606
permissive   398
permit   (**allow**)   37

permit   (**let**, v.i)   437
perpetual   200
perpetually   42
perplexed   194
perplexity   578
perseverance   538
persistent   168
persisting   430
personal   (**individual**)   397
personal effects   89
personality   500
persons   540
persuade   543
persuasive   790
pert   631
pertinent   319
pertness   160
perturb   26
peruse   594
pervert   700
perverted   205
pester   730
pet   v.   751
petite   447
petty   (**mean**, adj.ii)   474
petty   544
petulance   734
petulant   720
pew   648
phenomenon   365
phobia   642
phoney   292
physician   244
physiognomy   284
pick   167
picket   745
pickle   706
pick-pocket   739
picture   v.   545
picture   n.   546
picture   v.   (**think**)   742
picturesque   559
piebald   381
piece   99
pigmy   447
pile   371
pilfer   625
pilferer   739
pilgrimage   418

pile   457
pinch   625
pine for   (love)   458
pine for   (want)   780
pinion   308
pink   547
pinnace   112
pinnacle   750
pioneer   85
pint-sized   677
pipe   667
piquant   634
pique   698
piqued   614
pistol   360
pitch   744
pitch-black   103
pitchfork   744
pitiable   548
pitiful   548
pitiless   212
pivot   757
place   577
placid   136
plain   380
plainly   272
plain-spoken   328
plan   n.   (aim)   33
plan   v.   (intend)   406
plan   n.   (map)   469
plan   n.   549
planing   325
plant   577
plantation   797
platitude   573
plausible   598
play   333
playfulness   333
play on   25
pleasant   (nice)   508
pleasant   550
pleased as punch   344
pleased with oneself   190
pleasing   (nice)   508
pleasing   (pleasant)   550
pleasurable   266
pleasure   551
pledge   (swear, v.i)   723
pledge   n.   774

plentiful   489
plethora   276
pliable   682
pliant   682
plight   144
plight   552
plod   778
plodding   674
plot   549
plonk   577
plucky   114
plumage   308
plume   308
plump   304
plunder   n.   565
plunder   v.   625
plus   39
ply   766
poacher   739
pocket   (get)   339
podgy   304
point   285
pointless   553
point of view   45
point the finger at   104
poke   576
poker-faced   106
police   358
police station   412
polish   630
polished   680
polish off   423
polite   169
pollute   400
pompous   572
ponder   742
ponderous   789
pontificate   725
poor   554
poorly   387
popular   294
population   540
porcelain   210
pore over   594
portion   (bit)   99
portion   (part)   532
portly   304
portrait   546
portray   732

pose 577
position 577
positively 597
possess 370
possessions 89
possessive 414
possible 555
possibly (**maybe**) 472
possibly (**perhaps**) 542
post 654
postpone (**delay**) 237
postpone (**wait**) 776
postulate 88
pot-bellied 304
pot-belly 709
potentate 425
potential 2
pother 335
pottery 210
pouch 75
pounce 419
poverty-stricken 554
power 2
powerful 715
practicable 555
practical 767
practice (**habit**) 361
practice 556
practised (**experienced**) 280
practised 557
pragmatic 598
prairie 354
praise 322
prattle 725
preach 725
precedent 274
precipice 488
precise 204
precipitate 591
precipitately 367
precipitous 705
precocious 175
predicament 552
predict 558
predominant 464
predominantly 165
pre-eminent 693
prefer 167
preferably 404

preference 445
prejudiced 762
preliminary 670
premonition 310
preoccupied 759
preparatory 670
prepared (**alert**) 34
prepared (**ready**) 595
prepared to 5
preposterous 666
prescribe 23
present n. (**bonus**) 115
present n. (**gift**, n.i) 340
present v. (**give**) 343
present v. (**show**) 664
presentable 535
presentiment 310
present-day (**up-to-date**) 764
present-day (**modern**) 486
presently 688
preserve (**keep**) 422
press 751
press forward 576
pressing 765
prestige 293
presume 722
presumption 561
pretend 19
pretty (**lovely**) 459
pretty 559
prevailing 527
prevail upon 543
prevaricator 439
prevent 711
previous 326
previously 84
price 560
pride 561
primarily 465
primary 318
primed 595
primitive 637
primrose 802
principal 318
principally (**chiefly**) 165
principally (**mainly**) 465
principles 182
prison 412
prisoner 562

private 563
prize n.(i) 564
prize n.(ii) 565
probable (likely) 443
probable (possible) 555
probe 273
problem (case) 144
problem (puzzle) 578
probably (easily) 252
probably 566
procedure (plan) 549
procedure (practice) 556
proceedings 24
procession 567
proclaim 618
procrastinate 776
procure 339
prod 410
produce n. (goods) 350
produce v. (make) 466
productive 717
profession 799
proficient 280
profit 568
profitable 717
programme 549
progress 347
prohibit 711
projection 469
proletariat 587
prominence 293
prominent 150
promise (swear, v.i) 723
promise n. 774
promising 443
promote 117
prompt 403
promptly (hastily) 367
promptly 569
prone 321
pronounce 640
proof 570
propel 576
proper (acceptable) 12
proper (decent) 230
proper 571
property 89
prophesy 558
proportions 669

proposal 549
propose (intend) 406
propose (suggest) 719
proposition 716
prospect v. 282
prospect n. 773
prosperous 717
prostrate 321
protect (defend) 234
protect (guard) 358
protected 633
protective 140
protest 515
proud 572
proverb 573
provide 721
providing 385
province 603
provision 721
provisional 670
provoke 519
provoked 614
prowl 778
prudent 34
prying 521
pseudo 291
public 540
publication 116
publicize 117
publish 618
puerile 803
puff 124
puffy 724
pull 574
pull through (recover, v.ii) 600
pulpy 682
pulse 621
pulverize 241
pummel 377
punch 377
punctually 569
pungent 100
punt 112
puny 787
puppy-like 803
purchase 339
pure 575
purloin 625
purpose (aim) 33

purpose (**end**, n.ii) 262
purposeless 553
purse 75
pursue 157
push 576
put 577
put away 246
put back together 478
put down 581
put forward 719
put off 237
putrefy 627
putrid (**rotten**, adj.ii) 628
putrid (**smelly**) 678
put right 478
put up 131
put up with 37
puzzle 578
pyramid 753

quaff 246
quagmire 113
quail 208
quaint 714
quake 656
qualified 280
qualified for, be 240
qualm 579
quandary 552
quantity 44
quarrel 580
quarrel (**row**) 629
queer 518
quell 581
quench 582
query v. 61
query n. 583
quest 418
question (**ask**) 61
question 583
quibble 57
quick (**fast**) 302
quick 584
quick-witted 615
quiet (**calm**, adj.i) 136
quiet 585
quill 308
quip 417

quit 710
quite adv.(i) & (ii) 586
quiver 656
quiz 61
quotation 560

rabble (**crowd**) 211
rabble 587
race (**people**) 540
racket 509
radiant 125
radiate 658
radio 654
rage 725
ragged 411
raging (**angry**) 46
raging (**mad**) 462
ragtag and bobtail 587
raid 63
rail against 10
rain 588
raincoat 180
raise 441
raise aloft 441
raise high 441
ramble (**talk**) 725
ramble (**walk**) 778
rampart 779
ranch 300
rancid 691
random 589
range 488
rank adj.(i) & (ii) 590
rank (**smelly**) 678
ransack 651
ransom 613
rant 725
ranting 46
rap 377
rapacious (**greedy**, adj.i) 356
rapid 302
rapidity 696
rapids 623
rapier 426
rare 693
rarely 652
rash 591
rasp v. 630

reprimand (**scold**) 644
reproach 104
reproduce 611
reproduction (**likeness**) 444
reprove (**rebuke**) 599
reprove (**scold**) 644
repugnant 242
repulse 519
repulsive (**awful**, adj.ii) 70
repulsive (**ugly**) 758
reputation (**fame**) 293
reputation 612
repute 612
request v. 61
request n. 525
require 780
rescue 613
rescue (**save**, v.i) 638
resemble 32
resemblance 444
resent 86
resentful 614
resentful (**sulky**) 720
resentment 698
reserve 639
reserved 665
reservoir 197
residence 379
residents 540
resist openly 236
resolution 33
resolve 406
resourceful (**clever**) 175
resourceful 615
respect 21
respectable (**acceptable**) 12
respectable (**decent**) 230
respected 150
respectful 169
respecting (**about**, prep.i) 4
respecting (**concerning**) 191
respire 124
resplendent 224
respond 50
respond to 476
restate 611
restive 616
restless 616
restore (**mend**) 478

restore (**refresh**) 602
restore (**return**) 617
restrain 711
restraint 538
restricted 563
result 255
resuscitate 602
restyle 152
retail price 560
retail store 660
retain 370
retaliate 50
retell 611
reticent 665
retinue 567
retiring 665
retort 50
retract 3
retreat 617
retrieve (**recover**, v.i) 600
return (**profit**) 568
return 617
reveal 618
revealing 733
revengeful 614
revenue 568
revere 21
reverse 617
review v. (**assess**) 62
review v. 619
revile 10
revise (**read**) 594
revise 620
revitalize 602
revive 602
revoke 3
revolting 498
revolve 757
revolver 360
revulsion 198
reward 115
reword 611
rework 620
rewrite 620
rhythm 621
rich 622
riddle 578
ridged 411
ridiculous 666

safe adj. 633
safeguard 234
saffron 802
sag 247
saga 713
sagacious 795
saintly 348
saline 634
sallow (pale) 529
sallow (yellow) 802
salmon-pink 547
saloon 138
salty 634
salvage 638
same 635
sample 274
sanction (confirm) 193
sanction (let, v.i) 437
sanctioned 520
sandstorm 712
sandy 802
sanguine 601
sanity 481
sapphire 109
sarcastic 636
sardonic 636
satchel 75
satiated 332
satiny 680
satisfactory 508
satisfy (answer, v.ii) 51
satisfy (quench) 582
satisfy (supply) 721
satisfying 266
saturate 706
saturated 791
saunter 778
sauté 202
savage (fierce) 312
savage 637
savannah 354
save conj. (but) 135
save (rescue) 613
save v.(i) 638
save v.(ii) 639
savour 727
saw-toothed 411
say 640
scale 176

scan 594
scandalous 399
scanty 311
scarce 311
scarcely (hardly) 366
scarcely 641
scarcely any 311
scarcely ever 652
scare 642
scared 27
scarlet 601
scene 773
scenery 773
scent 643
sceptical 763
scheme v. 406
scheme n. 549
scheming (artful) 59
scheming (cunning) 214
scholarly 795
scholarship 428
school 728
schooling 428
schoolmaster 729
schoolmistress 729
schooner 659
science fiction 713
scimitar 426
scintillate 658
scintillating 127
scoff at 236
scold 644
scorn 198
scour 630
scoured 172
scourge 377
scowl 453
scraggy 740
scramble up 176
scrap 99
scrape (plight) 552
scrape (save, v.ii) 639
scraps 420
scratch 645
scrawl 800
scrawny 740
scream 646
screech 646
screen v. 375

set in motion   85
set out   (**define**)   235
set out   (**go**)   347
settee   151
settle   v.   231
settle   n.   648
set up   327
sever   215
severe   707
sexy   459
shabby   650
shack   379
shade   185
shadow   157
shady   676
shake   656
sham   v.   19
sham   adj.   291
shamble   778
shameful   (**disgraceful**)   242
shameful   657
shameless   775
shampoo   783
shanty   (**home**)   379
shanty   (**song**)   687
shapeless   76
sharp   (**clever**)   175
sharp   (**cold**)   183
sharp-witted   175
shatter   123
shed tears   213
sheer   705
shell out   697
sheltered   633
shelve   237
shield   (**defend**)   234
shield   (**guard**)   358
shiftless   435
shifty   (**artful**)   59
shifty   (**cunning**)   214
shimmer   658
shine   658
shiny   125
ship   v.   654
ship   n.   659
shipload   450
shire   381
shiver   656
shock   (**hair**)   362

shock   (**scare**)   642
shocking   242
shoddy   70
shop   660
shoplift   625
shoplifter   739
shore   661
short   677
short time ago, a   433
shortly   adv.(i) & (ii)   662
shortly   (**soon**)   688
shotgun   360
shoulder through   576
shout   663
shove   576
show   664
shower   n.   588
shower   v.   783
shrewd   214
shriek   (**laugh**)   434
shriek   (**scream**)   646
shrink   208
shrinking   665
shudder   656
shuffle   778
shun   504
shut   177
shy   adj.   665
shy   v.   744
shy away   245
sick   387
sickening   498
sickly   387
side   254
side-splitting   334
sidestep   245
sidle   778
sierra   488
sight   649
significant   790
silence   423
silky   680
silly   666
silvery   357
similar   635
similarity   444
simmer   202
simper   679
simple   675

simply 479
sincerely 755
sing 667
single out 167
singular 608
sip 246
sire 531
sit 668
situate 577
situation 144
size 669
sketch n. 546
sketch v. 732
sketchy 670
skewbald 381
skiff 112
skilful (**clever**) 175
skill 671
skim 594
skimming 325
skimpy 311
skinflint 482
skinny 740
skin-tight 746
sky-blue 109
skyscape 773
slack (**lazy**) 435
slack (**loose**) 456
slanderer 134
slap 377
slapdash 610
slash (**cut**) 215
slay 423
sleazy 650
sledge 771
sleek 680
sleep 672
slender 740
slice (**cut**) 215
slice (**part**) 532
slight 386
slim 740
sling 744
slink 778
slippery 676
slipshod 610
slit 215
sliver 99
slogan 673

sloop 112
sloppily 53
sloppy 480
slothful 435
slouch 247
slovenly 480
slow adj.(i) 674
slow adj.(ii) 675
slow up 237
slow-witted 675
sludgy 491
sluggish 435
sluice 623
slumber 672
slump 247
slushy 491
sly (**artful**) 59
sly (**cunning**) 214
sly 676
small 447
small 677
smallholding 300
small-minded 474
smart adj. 175
smart v. 383
smarting 689
smash 123
smashing 736
smash-up 206
smell a rat 722
smelly 678
smile 679
smilingly 345
smirk 679
smog 484
smoky 357
smooth (**rub**) 630
smooth 680
smother (**choke**) 166
smother (**quench**) 582
smug 190
smuggler 739
smutty (**naughty**, adj.ii) 502
smutty (**vulgar**) 775
snap (**break**) 123
snap (**say**) 640
snapshot 546
snare 146
snarled 490

successful 717
succour 374
succulent 238
sudden 584
suddenly 718
suffering 528
sufficient 267
suffocate 166
suggest (advise) 23
suggest 719
suggestive 733
suit 32
suitable (fitting) 319
suitable (good, adj.ii) 349
suitcase 75
sulky 720
sullen 720
sullied 103
sum 44
summarize 619
summit 488
sumptuous (magnificent) 463
sumptuous (rich) 622
sum up 619
sunder 215
sundry 468
sunless 183
sunny 174
sunrise 221
superabundance 276
superb 463
supercilious 572
superficial 670
supermarket 660
supersede 3
supple 30
supplement 393
supplementary, a 49
supply (heap) 371
supply 721
support (carry) 143
support (comfort) 187
suppose 359
supposing 385
supreme head 425
suppress (quell) 581
suppress (stop, v.ii) 711
surely (truly) 755
surf 786

surfeit 276
surge 323
surgeon 244
surliness 734
surly 499
surmise 359
surplus 276
surplus 568
surrender 1
surreptitious 704
surrounded by 43
survey 282
survive 703
suspect 722
suspend (delay) 237
suspend (hang) 363
suspicious (jealous) 414
suspicious (unsure) 763
swab 783
swagger 778
swamp 113
swampy 491
swap 277
sway 25
swear v.(i) & (ii) 723
sweepstake 564
swell 786
swift (fast) 302
swift (quick) 584
swiftness 696
swig 246
swill 246
swindle v. 159
swindle n. 229
swindler 739
swipe 625
switchblade 426
swivel 757
swollen 724
symmetrical 606
symmetry 526
sympathetic 508
synonymous 635
system 467
systematic 606

tabloid 506
tack 303
tackle 626

tactics   549
taint   400
take   (**accept**)   11
take   (**get**)   339
take advantage of   9
take a siesta   672
take heed   95
take home   339
take into custody   146
take on   11
take pleasure in   442
take advantage of   9
tale-bearer   134
talent   (**ability**)   2
talent   (**gift**, n.ii)   341
talented   175
talk   725
tally   32
tame   adj.(i) & (ii)   726
tangible   596
tangled   490
tank   771
tanker   659
tantrum   734
tap   377
tardy   432
tariff   560
tarnish   699
tarry   776
tart   691
task   798
taste   (**liking**)   445
taste   727
tasty   238
tattle   725
taunting   636
taut   746
tawny   802
taxi   138
teach   728
teacher   729
tear   171
tease   730
teasing   333
technique   467
tedious   118
teenage   803
teenager   121
telegraph   654

telescope   731
televise   654
tell   (**say**)   640
tell   732
telling   733
telling   (**weighty**)   790
temper   734
temperament   (**attitude**)   64
temperament   (**nature**)   500
tempest   712
tempo   621
tempt   (**lure**)   461
tempt   735
tender   (**boat**)   112
tender   (**gentle**)   338
tender   (**sore**)   689
tender-hearted   338
tenement   379
tepid   782
terminal   394
terminate   316
termination   261
terminus   261
terracotta   210
terra firma   429
terrain   429
terrible   307
terrific   736
terrified   27
terrifying   307
territory   603
terror   642
test   273
testament   530
testify   (**swear**, v.i)   723
testimony   774
tether   745
text   716
textbook   116
thatch   362
that is   497
that is to say   497
the drink   647
the latest thing   486
theme   716
then   (**afterwards**)   28
then   737
theory   384.
therefore   (**so**, conj.)   681

tornado   712
torrent   588
tortuous   396
toss   744
tossing   98
to some extent   686
tot   73
total   adj.   36
total   n.   44
totally   (**absolutely**)   8
totally   (**altogether**)   41
total war   781
totter   778
touch   (**affect**, v.ii)   26
touch   751
touch-and-go   655
touching   537
tough   752
tour   418
tournament   336
tow   574
tower   753
to whatever extent   382
toxic   305
track   157
tract   116
tractor   771
trade   v.   277
trade   n.   415
tradewind   794
trail   v.   157
trail   n.   643
trail up   176
train   (**procession**)   567
train   (**teach**)   728
train   (**vehicle**)   771
trained   (**efficient**)   256
trained   (**tame**, adj.i)   726
trainer   729
trait   155
tram   771
tramp   778
tranquil   136
transaction   24
transcribe   800
transferrable   147
transform   152
transformer   265
translucent   173

transmissible   147
transmit   143
transparent   173
transpire   364
transport   143
transversely   17
trash   420
travel   v.   347
tread   778
treasure   458
treatise   116
trek   418
tremble   656
trend-setter   (**fashion**, n.i)   301
tresses   362
tribe   424
tributary   623
trick   (**cheat**)   159
trick   754
trickle   323
tricky   214
tricolour   320
trifling   544
trilby   368
trill   667
trinket   232
trip   418
trivial   544
trolley   771
trophy   564
trouble   (**effort**)   257
trouble   (**care**)   139
troublesome   48
trounce   233
truck   771
trudge   778
truism   573
truly   (**indeed**)   395
truly   (**quite**, adv.i)   586
truly   (**really**)   597
truly   755
trumped up   292
trundle   576
trunk   120
truss   745
trust   87
trustworthy   607
trusty   562
truth   285

truthfully 755
try (**taste**) 727
try 756
tryst 477
tubby 304
tuck in 253
tug n. 112
tug v. 574
tumbler 346
tummy 709
tundra 354
tune 687
tunic 180
turbine 265
turf 353
turgid 724
turmoil 154
turn 757
turn a blind eye 386
turn into 81
turquoise 109
turret 753
tussle 313
tutor v. 728
tutor n. 729
twine up 176
twinge 528
twinkle 658
twist 90
twitch 656
type 424
typical (**average**) 67
typical (**ordinary**) 527

ugly 758
unadorned 105
unaffected 380
unbroken 200
unalloyed 575
unambitious 435
unassailable 633
unassuming 487
unattached 456
unavailing 768
unbelievable 283
unbending 707
unbiased (**fair**) 289

unblemished 541
unbroken (**continuous**) 200
unbroken (**flat**) 321
uncaring 372
unceasingly 42
uncertain 763
uncertainty 583
unchained 456
unchanged 405
unchanging (**even**) 270
unchanging (**same**) 635
uncivil 631
uncivilized 637
unclasped 456
unclear 391
unclothed 494
uncommon 714
unconcerned 759
unconditionally 8
unconfident 763
unconnected 456
unconsidered 589
uncontaminated 575
uncontrolled 591
unconventional 518
unconvinced 763
uncorrupted 172
uncouth 631
uncover 618
uncultivable 108
undamaged 405
undecided 763
undecorated 105
under 760
undercover 704
underfed 740
underhand 214
underline 259
underneath 760
understand (**know**, v.i) 427
understand 761
understanding 508
undertake 756
undertaking (**affair**) 24
undertaking (**vow**) 774
undertaking (**work**, n.i) 798
undeserved 762
undesignated 496
undisturbed 136

unstable 153
unstained 172
unsuitable 71
unsure 763
unsympathetic (**heartless**) 372
untamed 637
untidy 480
untied 456
untimely 71
untouched 405
untrue 292
untrustworthy 205
unusual (**odd**) 518
unusual (**strange**) 714
unvaried (**boring**) 118
unvaried (**even**) 270
unveil 664
unwanted 451
unwary 591
unwell 387
unwieldy (**awkward**, adj.i) 71
unwieldy (**weighty**, adj.i) 789
unwise 666
unworried 759
unyielding 707
upbraid (**rebuke**) 599
upbraid (**scold**) 644
update 620
upheaval 154
uphold 441
uplift 402
upright 421
uproar 509
upset 154
upshot 255
up-to-date (**modern**) 486
up-to-date 764
urchin 121
urge 23
urgent 765
usable 767
usage 361
use 766
useful (**convenient**) 201
useful 767
usefulness 770
useless 768
usual (**regular**) 605
usual 769

usually 522
utilize 766
utter 640
utterly 8

vacant 260
vacation 378
vague 287
vain 553
valiant 122
valid 596
validation 570
valuation 560
value 770
vandalize 699
vanity 561
vanquish (**defeat**) 233
vanquish (**quell**) 581
vapour 484
variable 153
variety 424
various 468
vast 97
vastness 692
vault 419
vaunting 111
veer 245
vehemently 251
vehicle 771
veil 375
veld 354
velocity 696
venal (**greedy**, adj.i) 356
vendetta 580
venerable 150
venerate 21
venom 698
venomous 305
ventilate 618
venture 756
verge 254
verify 193
versed 557
very (**so**, adj.i) 681
very 772
vessel (**container**) 197
vessel (**ship**) 659
vex 730

wrangle (**row**) 629
wrath 734
wreck 241
wretched 548
write 800
writing 801

yacht 112
yank 574
yearn for (**love**) 458
yearn for (**want**) 780
yell 663
yellow 802
yelp 646
yet 135
yield v. 343

yield n. 568
yoke 745
young 803
youth 121
youthful 803

zealot 295
zealously 251
zenith 750
zephyr 794
zestful 373
zigzag v. 90
zigzag adj. 396
zone 603
zoo 804
zooming 325